WALK WITH GOD

Gloria Copeland

Kenneth Copeland Publications
Fort Worth, Texas

Walk With God

ISBN 0-88114-985-3   30-0521

All scripture is from the *King James Version* unless otherwise noted.

Kenneth Copeland Publications
Fort Worth, Texas 76192-0001

Contents

Introduction

Through the years as Ken and I have traveled across the country, we've often heard, "Churches are failing. Believers are failing. People who know God's Word are failing. What is wrong?"

The answer is simple: God's people are not walking in obedience.

If believers are failing, it is because they are not obeying God's Word. If faith people are failing, it's because they are not walking in faith. And some Christians are failing because they are ignorant of what His Word says about them. Still others are trying to hang on to the world's way with one hand and the things of God with the other. It is easy to "talk the talk," but it takes dedication to "walk the walk."

God's deepest desire has always been to fellowship with His children, but He is hindered so often because of our disobedience, just as He was in the Garden of Eden because of Adam's disobedience.

As the Body of Christ, we have come to a place where we must determine to fellowship with God and obey Him *all* the time. We must get serious about our walk with God. Even though Jesus paid the price for our salvation, we could not be born again until we made ourselves obedient to the gospel. The laws of the Spirit apply to every aspect of our existence—and in every area that we refuse to be obedient, we shut the door to His blessings in that area. We must allow God to occupy the number one place in our lives.

You may say, "But there is so much pressure on me. Everybody around me is living the other way. How can I live for God? What can I do that's important to God? I'm just one person."

The days are short; the times are evil. Satan knows his days are numbered, so he is doing everything he can to destroy the Church of Jesus Christ. You may only be one person, but every member of the Church of Jesus Christ has a part to play. There are no insignificant members in His Body. The Lord has a work for you to do, a special part for you to play, a place that only *you* can fill.

If you desire to be a part of that glorious Church when Jesus returns, put yourself in agreement with God and obey His Word. Commit to walking with Him.

"How can I do that?" you ask. Well, you can't outside the realm of obedience. Amos 3:3 says, *"Can two walk together, except they be agreed?"* You have to be in agreement with God if you want to walk with Him. You have to learn how to agree with His Word. You have to learn to make His thoughts your thoughts, His ways your ways.

You have to learn these things because He's not the one who needs to change. He can't change. He's perfect in every respect.

"Well, what can I do? How can I become more obedient to God? How can I change?"

The first step is to find out what God has to say about obedience. The importance of walking in obedience to God is emphasized throughout Scripture.

So come before the Word of God as a little child, as though you have never read or heard it before. Walk with me through the Word of God as we search the Scripture regarding obedience. Come ready to learn, ready to change, ready for your mind to be renewed. Come ready to obey!

Gloria Copeland

1

Old Testament Obedience

God has always desired a people who would choose to walk with Him, a people who would follow Him, a people who would come into agreement with Him, and walk with Him in the earth.

Generation after generation He has desired a people He could elevate to such a place that all the nations of the world would know that these are the people He has blessed.

But there's always been a problem. It existed in the Garden of Eden. It was in the children of Israel in the wilderness. And to a great extent, it's in the Church today. The problem? Disobedient people.

Walking the Walk

Just because you're born again, and heaven will be your home, you are not free from being obedient to God. More than ever, you should be obedient because now you don't have to walk in oldness of the letter—the Old Testament law. You can walk in obedience in newness of spirit. You've been reborn to be obedient.

Under the old covenant, the people weren't born to be obedient. They had to be obedient by keeping the Law diligently...with their souls—their minds, wills and emotions.

We're to keep God's Word not only with our souls, but with our hearts, our spirits. It's so much easier for us to be obedient to God than it was for them because we have a new heart, born again in the image and nature of God.

While we're still here on the earth, we have to do what we can for God. We have to be obedient and victorious in every area of our lives.

Jesus knew this when He was a man on the earth. He was raised among people who knew they had to obey the voice of God and keep His statutes.

He learned what the prophets of God said before Him and began a walk of perfect obedience.

Lessons in Obedience

Following Jesus' example, we will examine the lives of some Old Testament men who were faced with the choices of life or death, obedience or disobedience. We'll learn valuable lessons from their lives. Adam is our example of disobedience. Enoch, Noah, Abraham and Moses are good examples of obedience. We will see what choices they made, and what the consequences were.

Some of these Scripture passages may be familiar. You may have heard and read them many times, but I remind you of the Apostle Paul's words to the Corinthian church: *"Now these things befell them by way of a figure—as an example and warning [to us]; they were written to admonish and fit us for right action by good instruction..."* (1 Corinthians 10:11, *The Amplified Bible).*

These examples of men faithful to God will help inspire us to faithfulness in obeying Him. They reveal to us the victorious outcome of obedience. Or in Adam's case the disastrous outcome of disobedience. We will let these men, all of whom had a choice, encourage us to make the right choice. First we will look at Adam's downfall that came because of failure to do what God said.

Adam

And God said, Let us make man in our image, after our likeness: and let them have dominion over the fish of the sea, and over the fowl of the air, and over the cattle, and over all the earth, and over every creeping

thing that creepeth upon the earth (Genesis 1:26).

And the Lord God formed man of the dust of the
ground, and breathed into his nostrils the breath of
life; and man became a living soul (Genesis 2:7).

So God created man in his own image, in the image
of God created he him; male and female created he
them. And God blessed them, and God said unto
them, Be fruitful, and multiply, and replenish the
earth, and subdue it: and have dominion over the
fish of the sea, and over the fowl of the air, and over
every living thing that moveth upon the earth
(Genesis 1:27-28).

God created this man, named him Adam and gave him
dominion over the earth. Genesis 3:8 says that God and Adam
walked together in the cool of the day. God created Adam in
His exact likeness and image because He wanted Adam to be
on His level, able to walk and talk with Him in sweet fellowship. He offered Adam the very highest kind of life—to be His
family in the earth. Adam was instructed to subdue the earth
and replenish it with beings in his own image, which had
been created in God's image.

God gave only one requirement to Adam: *"Of every tree of
the garden thou mayest freely eat: But of the tree of the knowledge of good and evil, thou shalt not eat of it: for in the day that
thou eatest thereof thou shalt surely die"* (Genesis 2:16-17).

The only thing God required from Adam was *obedience,* but
the day came when he chose to exercise his own will and disobey God's command.

The moment that Adam ate of the forbidden tree, the very
life of God was cut off from him. That fellowship, that intimate communication and relationship he had so enjoyed
with God, was over. He was immediately separated from God
and died spiritually just as God had warned. Separation from
God is spiritual death. He became separated from his spiritual
life source.

By disobeying God, Adam chose death as surely as if he had signed a legal document saying, "I choose death." Because of his disobedience, the future of the world was affected—all of Adam's seed were born into this world with the nature of sin instead of righteousness—with the nature of Satan instead of the nature of God. Adam committed high treason against God and Satan became his master. Disobedience and rebellion became dominant in the earth. Sin put man in opposition to the thoughts and ways of God. Thus, through one man's disobedience, death reigned. *"For if by one man's offence death reigned by one; much more they which receive abundance of grace and of the gift of righteousness shall reign in life by one, Jesus Christ"* (Romans 5:17).

Something had to be done. God had given Adam dominion over the earth and Adam, by disobedience, had made himself subject to and less powerful than God's enemy, Satan. It would take time for God to provide the way back for man to come into union and agreement with Him again. But He would do it.

Even in the Garden, God knew what price He must pay. But He was willing to pay it to get His family back. He said to Satan: *"I will put enmity between thee and the woman, and between thy seed and her seed; it shall bruise thy head, and thou shalt bruise his heel"* (Genesis 3:15). He was willing to sacrifice His only Son to bring man back into fellowship with Himself: *"For God so loved the world, that he gave his only begotten Son, that whosoever believeth in him should not perish, but have everlasting life"* (John 3:16).

Adam met disaster because of disobedience. He was separated from the life of God. He was exiled from the perfect environment God had created for him.

And to Adam, God said, "Because you listened to your wife and ate the fruit when I told you not to, I have placed a curse upon the soil. All your life you will struggle to extract a living from it. It will grow

thorns and thistles for you, and you shall eat its grasses. All your life you will sweat to master it, until your dying day. Then you will return to the ground from which you came. For you were made from the ground, and to the ground you will return."

...Then the Lord said, "Now that the man has become as we are, knowing good from bad, what if he eats the fruit of the Tree of Life and lives forever?" So the Lord God banished him forever from the Garden of Eden, and sent him out to farm the ground from which he had been taken. Thus God expelled him, and placed mighty angels at the east of the Garden of Eden, with a flaming sword to guard the entrance to the Tree of Life (Genesis 3:17-19, 22-24, *The Living Bible*).

Moreover, because of Adam's disobedience, sin and death passed to all of Adam's offspring, *"For as by one man's disobedience many were made sinners..."* (Romans 5:19).

What a price Adam and his family paid because of disobedience!

Enoch

And Enoch walked [in habitual fellowship] with God; and he was not, for God took him [home with Him] (Genesis 5:24, *The Amplified Bible*).

Enoch diligently heeded the voice of the Lord. In the New Testament book of Hebrews, he is described clearly:

By faith Enoch was conveyed to another place [namely, heaven], with the result that he did not see death, and he was not found because God had conveyed him to another place [heaven]. For before his removal [from earth to heaven] he had witness borne

**[to him], that testimony still being on record, to the
effect that he pleased God (Hebrews 11:5, *Wuest
Expanded Translation).***

Enoch walked with God. He pleased God. And then God took
him! Did you get that? Enoch walked so closely with God that
one day he just didn't come back! He was so close to God,
because of his obedience to God, that he didn't die a natural
death. He was lifted right into heaven.

Can you, as a new creature in Christ Jesus, say you have
pleased God and walked with Him so closely that you could be
lifted right up to heaven? If you are born again and alive when
Jesus returns, that is what is in store for you. Enoch, being
translated out of an evil world, typifies the saints (the glorious
Church) who will soon be removed from this earth, who will be
changed from mortality to immortality, without their bodies
passing through the grave (1 Corinthians 15:51-54).

Enoch is an inspiring example of walking with God.

Noah

Throughout the ages God's Spirit continually has striven
with a wicked people. At more than one point God was close
to annihilating the entire human race. Noah is an example of
how obedience saved mankind from being destroyed from
the face of the earth.

**And God saw that the wickedness of man was great
in the earth, and that every imagination of the
thoughts of his heart was only evil continually.**

**And it repented the Lord that he had made man on
the earth, and it grieved him at his heart.**

**And the Lord said, I will destroy man whom I have
created from the face of the earth; both man, and
beast...for it repenteth me that I have made them
(Genesis 6:5-7).**

But He remembered Noah. Noah became the man of the hour. *"But Noah found grace in the eyes of the Lord....Noah was a just man and perfect in his generations, and Noah walked with God"* (Genesis 6:8-9).

One man saved the human race—one man who dared to be obedient to God. Noah was the last righteous man on earth. God waited as long as He could. He waited until there was only one righteous man left. Think about that!

Thank God, Noah did not do like many people today and say, "There is just too much pressure for me to live in this evil generation. After all, I'm only one man. What can I do?"

Noah heard the voice of the Lord and he obeyed. God said, "Build an ark," so Noah built an ark. The people around him scoffed and made fun of him, but that did not stop Noah. Walking in obedience to God was more important to him than what other people had to say.

In Genesis 7, God said to Noah, *"Come thou and all thy house into the ark; for thee have I seen righteous before me in this generation"* (verse 1). *"And Noah did according unto all that the Lord commanded him"* (verse 5). Because of one man's obedience, the entire human race and the animal kingdom were saved from destruction.

> **And they went into the ark with Noah, two and two of all flesh, in which there was the breath and spirit of life. And they that entered, male and female of all flesh, went in as God had commanded [Noah]; and the Lord shut him in and closed [the door] round about him (Genesis 7:15-16, *The Amplified Bible*).**

The future of the race of man was in Noah's hands. He was faithful to do all that God asked of him. He and his family were supernaturally preserved because he obeyed God.

While we are on this earth, evil circumstances will try to rush in like a flood and overcome us. But as long as we are walking in obedience, God will make an ark around us for protection. He will shut the door to evil and nothing can open it. The same principle will work in reverse when we disobey God. The door will close, only this time in front of us, keeping us outside, unable to live the kind of life God wants us to live.

Abraham

Faith is believing God's Word enough to act on it. James 2:26 says, *"...faith without works is dead also."* *Weymouth's New Testament* translation says, *"For just as a human body without a spirit is lifeless, so also faith is lifeless without obedience."* Faith is acting on God's Word.

Abraham is a great example of obedience and faith. In Genesis 12:1, God told Abraham to get out of his country and go away from his relatives to a land that He would show him:

> **Now the Lord had said unto Abram, Get thee out of thy country, and from thy kindred, and from thy father's house, unto a land that I will show thee:**
> **And I will make of thee a great nation, and I will bless thee, and make thy name great; and thou shalt be a blessing.**

Verse 4 of this chapter then says, *"So Abram departed, as the Lord had spoken unto him...."*

When the Lord told Abraham that he would have seed as numerous as the stars, the Bible says, *"And he believed in the Lord; and he counted it to him for righteousness"* (Genesis 15:6). Abraham and Sarah had never been able to have children, even in their youth. The same day God promised him seed, He made a covenant with Abraham (whose name at the time was Abram) declaring *"unto thy seed have I given this land..."* (Genesis 15:18).

Later God changed his name from Abram to Abraham which meant "father of many nations." Therefore, every time Abraham declared his new name saying, "I am Abraham," he was declaring, "I am the father of many nations!"

Isaac was the result of Abraham's believing what God said to him, even though it was a natural impossibility for him to have a son. Romans 4:3 says, *"...Abraham believed God and it was counted unto him for righteousness."*

For the promise, that he should be the heir of the world, was not to Abraham, or to his seed, through the law, but through the righteousness of faith.

Therefore it is of faith, that it might be by grace; to the end the promise might be sure to all the seed; not to that only which is of the law, but to that also which is of the faith of Abraham; who is the father of us all,

(As it is written, I have made thee a father of many nations,) before him whom he believed, even God, who quickeneth the dead, and calleth those things which be not as though they were.

Who against hope believed in hope, that he might become the father of many nations, according to that which was spoken, So shall thy seed be.

And being not weak in faith, he considered not his own body now dead, when he was about an hundred years old, neither yet the deadness of Sarah's womb:

He staggered not at the promise of God through unbelief; but was strong in faith, giving glory to God;

And being fully persuaded that, what he had promised, he was able also to perform (Romans 4:13, 16-21).

Abraham's obedience was promoted by his faith! Because he believed God he was able to hope when, in the natural, there was no hope that he would become the father of many nations. He didn't consider his own body, even though naturally speaking it was too old to produce children. Or that Sarah was not only past childbearing age, but also that she had never been able to bear children.

But God gave Abraham a promise. God made a covenant with him and that is what Abraham believed. In other words, Abraham didn't believe what he saw, but he believed what God said. The Word says he did not *"stagger at the promise of God."* He did not give place to unbelief. He was strong in faith and fully persuaded that God was able to perform what He had promised.

Throughout his life, God appeared to Abraham at different times and told him exactly what to do. Genesis 17:1-2 says:

> **And when Abram was ninety years old and nine, the Lord appeared to Abram, and said unto him, I am the Almighty God; walk before me, and be thou perfect [upright].**
> **And I will make my covenant between me and thee, and will multiply thee exceedingly.**

So Abraham obeyed God's voice and followed His directions. The following passage from *The Amplified Bible* is a picture of Abraham's *total obedience* to the Father:

> **[Urged on] by faith Abraham when he was called, obeyed and went forth to a place which he was destined to receive as an inheritance; and he went, although he did not know or trouble his mind about where he was to go.**
> **[Prompted] by faith he dwelt as a temporary resident in the land which was designated in the promise [of God, though he was as a stranger] in a strange country, living in tents with Isaac and Jacob, fellow heirs with him of the same promise.**
> **For he was waiting expectantly and confidently, looking forward to the city which has fixed and firm foundations, whose Architect and Builder is God (Hebrews 11:8-10, *The Amplified Bible*).**

By the supernatural power of God Sarah bore Abraham a son named Isaac. God gave Abraham the ultimate test as a father: to offer up his son Isaac on the altar. Look at this through Abraham's eyes for a moment. Isaac was the son through whom he was to be the father of many nations. How could he do it? There was only one way—by faith.

By faith Abraham, when he was put to the test— that is, while the testing of his faith was still in progress—had already brought Isaac for an offering; he who had gladly received and welcomed [God's] promises was ready to sacrifice his only son,
Of whom it was said, Through Isaac shall your descendants be reckoned.
For he reasoned that God was able to raise [him] up even from among the dead. Indeed in the sense that Isaac was figuratively dead (potentially sacrificed), he did [actually] receive him back from the dead (Hebrews 11:17-19, *The Amplified Bible*).

Just as Abraham raised the knife to slay Isaac, the angel of the Lord called out to him and said, *"Lay not thine hand upon the lad, neither do thou any thing unto him: for now I know that thou fearest God, seeing thou hast not withheld thy son, thine only son from me"* (Genesis 22:12).
Then Abraham saw a ram caught in a thicket. He took the ram and offered it as a sacrifice to the Lord in place of his son. God found in Abraham a man who would obey Him to the degree of giving up his son.
Through Abraham's life we see a picture of God's love for you and me. Just as Abraham didn't withhold his son from God, neither did God withhold His only begotten Son, Jesus, from us. He sent Jesus into the world and allowed Him to die on the cross so the world could be redeemed. And just as Abraham received back his son from the dead, God received back His only begotten Son when Jesus was raised from the dead.

Just as Abraham demonstrated faith as a father, so Isaac demonstrated faith as a son—willing to be offered as a sacrifice without a struggle. He was not a small child, he could have protested. But he had been trained in the way he should go—to *obey* his father in *all* things.

During his life, the Lord spoke to him as He had to his father Abraham. The Lord appeared to Isaac when he was grown, years after he was spared his life:

> **Go not down into Egypt; dwell in the land which I shall tell thee of: Sojourn in this land, and I will be with thee, and will bless thee; for unto thee, and unto thy seed, I will give all these countries, and I will perform the oath which I sware unto Abraham thy father; And I will make thy seed to multiply as the stars of heaven, and will give unto thy seed all these countries; and in thy seed shall all the nations of the earth be blessed; Because that Abraham obeyed my voice, and kept my charge, my commandments, my statutes, and my laws (Genesis 26:2-5).**

God performed His oath to Isaac because Abraham had obeyed His voice and kept His commandments. Obedience was the condition of the oath. Had Abraham not obeyed God, He would not have fulfilled His promise. Had Isaac not obeyed God, disobedience would have stopped the promise in his life.

Isaac and his seed were Abraham's seed and heirs according to the promise. If we are in Christ, we are also heirs according to the promise. The Apostle Paul wrote to the churches of Galatia:

> **Christ hath redeemed us from the curse of the law, being made a curse for us: for it is written, Cursed is every one that hangeth on a tree: That the blessing of Abraham might come on the Gentiles through Jesus**

Christ; that we might receive the promise of the Spirit through faith....

For ye are all the children of God by faith in Christ Jesus. For as many of you as have been baptized into Christ have put on Christ. There is neither Jew nor Greek, there is neither bond nor free, there is neither male nor female: for ye are all one in Christ Jesus. And if ye be Christ's, then are ye Abraham's seed, and heirs according to the promise (Galatians 3:13-14, 26-29).

Jesus came to redeem Abraham's seed. God sees the Church, as well as Abraham's natural descendants, as that seed. We have been grafted in through faith in Jesus Christ, the Anointed. It is our blood-bought right through Him.

However, our obedience determines how much of Abraham's blessing is manifested in our lives. That is a choice we must make. Am I going to be faithful to God and obey Him? Yes! At all costs!

Moses—the Deliverer

Moses is an exciting example of one who dared to obey God. The hand of God was upon him from birth. He performed many miracles in the life of Moses during his 120-year walk on the earth.

It was a miracle when the Egyptian princess retrieved 3-month-old Moses from a tiny ark of bulrushes on the edge of the Nile River.

It was a miracle when the princess, knowing Moses to be Hebrew, adopted him at the very time the Pharaoh decreed all male Hebrew babies to be killed.

It was a miracle that Moses' adoptive mother chose his natural mother to nurse him in her own home.

Later, as an adult, Moses killed an Egyptian for beating a Hebrew slave and fled into Egypt to settle in the land of Midian. There he had his first encounter with God.

Leading the Children of Israel

The angel of the Lord appeared to him and said:

> **I am the God of thy father, the God of Abraham, the
> God of Isaac, and the God of Jacob. And Moses hid his
> face; for he was afraid to look upon God.**
>
> **And the Lord said, I have surely seen the affliction
> of my people which are in Egypt, and have heard
> their cry by reason of their taskmasters; for I know
> their sorrows;**
>
> **And I am come down to deliver them out of the
> hand of the Egyptians, and to bring them up out of
> that land unto a good land and a large, unto a land
> flowing with milk and honey; unto the place of the
> Canaanites, and the Hittites, and the Amorites, and
> the Perizzites, and the Hivites, and the Jebusites
> (Exodus 3:6-8).**

In the next verses, God told Moses to go back to Egypt and
lead the children of Israel out of bondage. God gave him
detailed instructions about what to do and what to say to
Pharaoh and the Israelites. After some protest concerning his
suitability for the job, Moses obeyed God and was faithful. His
obedience brought results (Hebrews 3:5). (One exception to
this is found in Numbers 20. It kept Moses from entering into
the Promised Land.)

When the Israelites were delivered safely out of Egypt
and were camped in the wilderness, God called Moses to
Mount Sinai and said:

> **Thus shalt thou say to the house of Jacob, and tell
> the children of Israel;**
>
> **Ye have seen what I did unto the Egyptians, and
> how I bare you on eagles' wings, and brought you
> unto myself.**

Now therefore, if ye will obey my voice indeed, and keep my covenant, then ye shall be a peculiar treasure unto me above all people: for all the earth is mine:
And ye shall be unto me a kingdom of priests, and an holy nation. These are the words which thou shalt speak unto the children of Israel (Exodus 19:3-6).

God said if they would obey His voice, they would be His peculiar treasure in the earth—a nation set apart from all others, set on high above all the earth. God wanted Israel to be a nation of priests unto Him. He wanted to set them apart, so He could come into their midst and live among them. They were to be His special treasure.

You can see throughout the history of the nation of Israel that when Israel served Him with their whole heart—in obedience—He was wholly and totally God to them. He performed in their lives, whether it was with signs and wonders, with miracles, or whether it was with His angels going before them in battle. Whatever it took, when they served Him with their whole heart, He was there with His whole heart.

But when they were disobedient and didn't serve Him at all, He did not work in their lives.

Moses later said to the nation of Israel:

Behold, I have taught you statutes and ordinances as the Lord my God commanded me, that you should do them in the land which you are entering to possess.
So keep them and do them; for that is your wisdom and your understanding in the sight of the peoples, who, when they hear all these statutes, will say, Surely this great nation is a wise and understanding people (Deuteronomy 4:5-6, *The Amplified Bible*).

What was to make them a great nation, a wise and understanding people? *Keeping God's Word*—His ordinances and statutes.

It was keeping God's Word, His wisdom and understanding, that set Israel apart from other nations, showing them how to be the special people of God—a peculiar treasure. In Exodus 19:5 He said to Moses about Israel, *"Now therefore, if you will obey My voice in truth and keep My covenant, then you shall be My own peculiar possession and treasure from among and above all peoples; for all the earth is Mine" (The Amplified Bible).*

Later, in Deuteronomy 4:10, Moses said, *"...the Lord said unto me, Gather me the people together, and I will make them hear my words, that they may learn to fear me all the days that they shall live upon the earth, and that they may teach their children."*

When God said He wanted His people to fear Him, He did not mean for them to be afraid. He wanted them to have reverence and respect for Him, so they would be obedient to His Word. He did not want them to keep His Word just so He could have slaves. He knew that the only way they could be kept free from the curse on the earth was by obeying His Word.

Two Ways Israel Obeyed

God dealt with the Israelites in two ways: *He told them to keep His statutes and ordinances, and He told them to obey His voice.* Throughout all generations God never intended for His people to have only the written ordinances. If they would listen and obey the statutes and ordinances, they would also have His voice coming to them telling them what to do.

There were times when God spoke to Israel regarding specific situations. He told them what to do to get victory because He was their God and they were His people.

As long as they obeyed His voice, no enemy could stand before them. There might be many standing against them who were stronger in the natural realm, but that did not matter. As long as they obeyed the voice of the Lord, He moved supernaturally and they walked in victory because God was with them.

But this thing commanded I them, saying, Obey my voice, and I will be your God, and ye shall be my people: and walk ye in all the ways that I have commanded you, that it may be well unto you (Jeremiah 7:23).

The Father was continually telling Israel, "I will be your God. I will take care of you. I will meet all your needs. Just obey My voice and keep My Word." Isaiah 1:19 says, *"If ye be willing and obedient, ye shall eat the good of the land."*

In the same way, God can only go as far as we'll go with Him. God says in 1 Samuel 2:30, *"...them that honour me I will honour, and they that despise me shall be lightly esteemed."* How much you honor God in your life is how much God can honor you. Whatever area you hold back from Him, in whatever area you are disobedient, that is the area He can't bless. You've closed the door to Him in that area because of your disobedience. As we continue our study of obedience, we'll see that all through His Word God makes it very clear that if we want things to go well for us in this earth **we must choose to obey what He says.** God's way is the only way that liberates us from bondage into victory.

2

God Gives Us a Choice

God has always had to deal with a disobedient people. That has been His reward for His goodness and His mercy. He called out to generation after generation in love and mercy:

> **...Hear ye the words of this covenant, and do them. For I earnestly protested unto your fathers in the day that I brought them up out of the land of Egypt, even unto this day, rising early and protesting, saying, Obey my voice (Jeremiah 11:6-7).**

"I earnestly protested and pleaded with the fathers. I rose up early and told them to obey My voice." That is what God has done through the generations. He has continually tried to get His very best to His people, His special treasure.

He said, "I rose up early. I protested. I pleaded. I proclaimed, 'Obey My voice.'"

"Yet they obeyed not, nor inclined their ear, but walked every one in the imagination of their evil heart" (Jeremiah 11:8).

Let's look at Deuteronomy 5:29. Here the heart of God is saying once again, *"O that there were such an heart in them, that they would fear me, and keep all my commandments always, that it might be well with them, and with their children for ever!"*

This is the heart of God yearning over His special people, yearning over the people He formed for Himself. Although we are not in the same position as Israel was, God is in the same position with us where our obedience to the new covenant is concerned.

> **For I will take you from among the heathen, and gather you out of all countries, and will bring you into your own land.**

Then will I sprinkle clean water upon you, and ye shall be clean: from all your filthiness, and from all your idols, will I cleanse you.

A new heart also will I give you, and a new spirit will I put within you: and I will take away the stony heart [of death] out of your flesh, and I will give you an heart of flesh.

And I will put my spirit within you, and cause you to walk in my statutes, and ye shall keep my judgments, and do them.

And ye shall dwell in the land that I gave to your fathers; and ye shall be my people, and I will be your God (Ezekiel 36:24-28).

He said He would put a new heart in them. You and I have that new heart if we've made Jesus Lord of our lives. We not only have a new heart, but we also have God's Spirit dwelling in us to teach us to walk in His ways and give us individual guidance. When we come before the Lord on that great day for our rewards, we will have no excuse for not fulfilling His will. He has put a new spirit in us. His Spirit within us teaches us, counsels us and manifests the presence of Jesus in us.

The Cost of an Un-renewed Mind

I want you to see some things that have cost us God's best. We have had problems in our lives because our minds were not renewed to the goodness of God.

Proverbs 19:3 in *The Amplified Bible* says, *"The foolishness of man subverts his way [ruins his affairs]; then his heart is resentful and frets against the Lord."* This is so true. By going our own way, we get ourselves into trouble. Then we say, "Why did You do this to me, God?"

If we have continual defeat, God is not the one who has failed. We are the ones who have missed it. God's Word works. But if we walk in darkness, instead of in the light of His Word,

God's blessings will be hindered. The Church as a whole has done this. The Church has known so little about the truth of God. We have been just barely in the spiritual twilight zone when we could have been walking in the light. But God is not at fault.

Long ago when I first began to walk in faith, I learned that no matter what it looks like or what people tell me about their problems and their situations, God is not the one who has failed.

Early in his ministry Ken conducted a meeting in what at that time was the largest church he had ever preached in. This church had a member who had died of an incurable disease.

When Ken preached the Word, the integrity of God's Word, that you can count on God's Word, that faith works, the church members said, "Well it didn't work here!"

Maybe they didn't say it in those particular words, but that in essence is what they said. They let us know that a man in their congregation had done everything he was supposed to— and he still died. They told us a number of things regarding his spiritual life. They mentioned that his confessions were good and so on.

So what were these people really saying? "That this man was right, and God was wrong."

In Malachi we see God speaking strong words to Israel regarding this:

> **Your words have been stout against me, saith the Lord. Yet ye say, What have we spoken so much against thee?**
> **Ye have said, It is vain to serve God: and what profit is it that we have kept his ordinance, and that we have walked mournfully before the Lord of hosts? (Malachi 3:13-14).**

"Your words are stout against Me!" God says.

Well, this really bothered me. I mean, I was new at this and they were telling me that he had done *all* the right things.

They said he was a faith man. And he died! He was acting on the Word. And he died!

Have you ever heard that? Or been faced with that situation in your church, your family?

Well, the Lord taught me a great deal out of that situation. Another man for whom I have great respect said that he had gone to pray for this man. He went every day for a while and interceded for him. And he prayed the presence of Jesus into the man's room.

When Jesus appeared in that room the man who was dying jumped out of bed (he couldn't get out of bed by himself before) and knelt at Jesus' feet. As Jesus reached out to touch the man, he pulled away and dropped back.

He began to say, "I can't. I can't. I'm just not worthy."

Now the man who had been interceding was watching all of this, and he turned his gaze to Jesus. Jesus looked back at him and said, "See there, he won't let Me heal him."

Do you see what happened here? No doubt this was a good man. He had loved and served God, but religious tradition held him captive. Those church members were just sure he had done everything right. And maybe he did—except have his mind renewed to the Word of God. It's so important that we receive Who God really is—a God of mercy and compassion, a God Whose will is to heal and deliver and set free.

You have to trust God. Don't shut Him off in your mind with traditions of men, unbelief, fear and sin. If you let sin or unbelief condemn you so that you don't have any faith that God will move on your behalf, God can't help you. You shut Him off. The man said, "I can't receive. I'm too unworthy." Pentecostal, religious tradition kept him from receiving the power of God, even though Jesus was in his room to heal him.

I learned something very valuable from Jesse Winley, a great pastor from Harlem. "Don't ever put the righteousness of God up against anybody." That's good advice. God is never wrong. If things aren't working, we need to consider our ways, not God's. If we are disobedient, we need to make adjustments. If not, we need to walk by faith and not by sight until circumstances change.

Which Group Are You In?

And now we call the proud happy; yea, they that work wickedness are set up; yea, they that tempt God are even delivered.

Then they that feared the Lord spake often one to another: and the Lord hearkened, and heard it, and a book of remembrance was written before him for them that feared the Lord, and that thought upon his name.

And they shall be mine, saith the Lord of hosts, in that day when I make up my jewels; and I will spare them, as a man spareth his own son that serveth him.

Then shall ye return, and discern between the righteous and the wicked, between him that serveth God and him that serveth him not (Malachi 3:15-18).

The Lord hears when we talk to one another. He knows those who have respect and honor for Him. And He knows those who don't.

You can be in either group. We can be in the first group who has words that are stout against God. Or, we can be in the second group who fears God and speaks often about His goodness and His mercy. God told Israel in Exodus 19:5 if they would obey His voice and keep His covenant, they would be His *peculiar treasure,* or His *special treasure,* above all others in the earth. Here He refers to them as jewels. We think of treasure as gold and jewels. God's treasure is an obedient people. He paves His streets with gold, but He is able to achieve His dream for His family with a people who know and obey Him. You can be that treasure to Him. It is your choice.

You have to be willing *and* obedient in order to walk in victory (Isaiah 1:19). If you are just talking a good game, but not doing the Word, you are not being willing and obedient. You have to be willing and obedient to walk in the blessing of God.

Isaiah 3 shows us the contrast between the righteous and the wicked. (Remember, God does not condemn the righteous with the wicked. He appeared to the righteous Lot and got him out of Sodom and Gomorrah.)

"Say ye to the righteous, that it shall be well with him: for they shall eat the fruit of their doings. Woe unto the wicked! it shall be ill with him: for the reward of his hands shall be given him" (Isaiah 3:10-11).

God makes a difference between the righteous and the wicked, between the obedient and the disobedient. He is no respecter of persons (Acts 10:34), but He is a respecter of obedience and faith. He makes a difference between those who obey Him and those who do not.

The whole world could be in trouble and without any resources or abilities, while the Church—if we are obedient to God—would have plenty. Psalm 91:7 says, *"A thousand shall fall at thy side, and ten thousand at thy right hand; but it shall not come nigh thee."*

The blessings of God cannot flow to us when we are living in disobedience, even if we are born-again, Spirit-filled Christians. Because of a low level of obedience and spiritual maturity, the Church has just barely scratched the surface of the blessings of God.

God wants us to live in the earth like we were *already* in heaven. Jesus taught the disciples to pray *"Thy will be done in earth, as it is in heaven"* (Matthew 6:10). Deuteronomy 11 talks about the Lord giving *days of heaven upon the earth.* Wherever we walk, the kingdom of heaven should be manifested and in control. In many ways we are like little children, but we are growing and beginning to hear and to see the hope of our calling, and our inheritance in the saints in light (Ephesians 4:4; Colossians 1:12).

We already are born again. We are created in the image of God. We are citizens of that place called heaven. The kingdom of God is in us. The Spirit of God lives in us. He is here to take dominion now. Yet, if we do not walk with Him, obey Him and get our minds renewed to what He says, we give Him no place to move in our lives. We shut Him out and do not allow Him to take dominion in the earth through us. The dominion Jesus exercises in the earth is through His Body. He is the Head; we are the Body.

God has always desired to do mighty things in the earth, to overwhelm this world with His presence, to dwell in the midst of His people. He has always desired to manifest Himself. He has been waiting generation after generation for a people who would find out what He is like, believe His Word and dare to walk in it—a people who would know Him and comprehend Him, a people who would walk and talk and act like the Father and the Son.

May He grant you out of the rich treasury of His glory to be strengthened and reinforced with mighty power in the inner man by the (Holy) Spirit [Himself]— indwelling your innermost being and personality.

May Christ through your faith [actually] dwell— settle down, abide, make His permanent home—in your hearts! May you be rooted deep in love and founded securely on love,

That you may have the power and be strong to apprehend and grasp with all the saints (God's de- voted people, the experience of that love) what is the breadth and length and height and depth [of it];

[That you may really come] to know—practically, through experience for yourselves—the love of Christ, which far surpasses mere knowledge (with- out experience); that you may be filled (through all your being) unto all the fullness of God—[that is] may have the richest measure of the divine Presence, and become a body wholly filled and flooded with God Himself!

Now to Him Who, by (in consequence of) the [action of His] power that is at work within us, is able to [carry out His purpose and] do superabundantly, far over and above all that we [dare] ask or think— infinitely beyond our highest prayers, desires, thoughts, hopes or dreams—

To Him be glory in the church and in Christ Jesus throughout all generations, for ever and ever. Amen—so be it (Ephesians 3:16-21, *The Amplified Bible*).

I believe with all my heart that His Church is rising up glorious in our day. His Body is coming to the place for which He has waited thousands of years. As we make ourselves available to God and obey Him, He will be able to manifest Himself in the earth as He has yearned to do.

So choose to be in the right group. Join in with those who fear God, who speak of His goodness and mercy, who honor and respect Him. Choose to allow Him in every part of your life...and watch His goodness unfold!

3

Jesus Our Example

If you want to walk in obedience and receive God's goodness, I have good news for you. God *wants* to be God to you in a very personal and intimate way. He *wants* to be God in the Church. He *wants* to be God in your individual life. But He can only be God to you as far as you will follow Him.

As we have already learned God waited and waited for a people who would be obedient to Him, so that He could be God to them, manifesting His presence and glory. Finally, in the New Testament, one man fulfilled His call. One man was *absolutely* obedient. His Name is Jesus.

Jesus, the Son of God, came into the world to fulfill the perfect will of God. He stripped Himself of His heavenly privileges and was born of a woman. He took upon Himself flesh. The Holy Spirit hovered over Mary and conceived in her a holy thing. Because God was His Father, and not man, Jesus was born without sin.

The life of God was in Him instead of spiritual death. But Jesus did not just come into this world saying, "Look at Me—I'm the Son of Almighty God," and then live anyway He wanted. The thing that set Jesus apart and qualified Him to pay the price was His living as a man without sin. Yet when the time came, He was willing to lay down His own life and take sin into Himself for you and me. *"For he hath made him to be sin for us, who knew no sin; that we might be made the righteousness of God in him"* (2 Corinthians 5:21).

Had Jesus lived in the earth after His own will, He would never have gone to the cross. But Jesus did not live in the earth after His own will. When faced with death—separation from God—He changed His will in the Garden of Gethsemane to agree with God's will. Why? Because He knew the scriptures. He knew the Spirit of God. He knew His Father. He had the knowledge of God Who said, "Keep My statutes and ordinances. Keep My Word and obey My voice."

Do God's Will

"Then answered Jesus and said unto them, Verily, verily, I say unto you, The Son can do nothing of himself, but what he seeth the Father do: for what things soever he doeth, these also doeth the Son likewise" (John 5:19).

Jesus said He could do nothing of Himself. He did not try. He did not even want to do anything of Himself. He did only what He saw the Father do.

In John 5:30 Jesus said it again:

I am able to do nothing from Myself—independently, of My own accord—but as I am taught by God and as I get His orders. [I decide as I am bidden to decide. As the voice comes to Me, so I give a decision.] Even as I hear, I judge and My judgment is right (just, righteous), because I do not seek or consult My own will—I have no desire to do what is pleasing to Myself, My own aim, My own purpose—but only the will and pleasure of the Father Who sent Me *(The Amplified Bible).*

Jesus obeyed the Father. He did not make His own decisions, but lived absolutely obedient to the voice of God. He was totally submitted to His Father.

You see, Jesus understood the difference between following after the soul (mind, will, emotions) and following after the spirit. He could have followed after His soul, but He counted that as nothing. Compared to walking after the spirit, that is exactly what walking after the soul is—nothing. You and I just do not know enough to walk after our natural thinking. That is why God gave us His Holy Spirit—to teach us to think like He thinks, to reveal His Word to us (Isaiah 55:7-11; John 14:26).

Jesus knew the written statutes and ordinances of the scriptures, but He also knew and operated by the voice of the Lord. He spent time in prayer with the Father: "What shall I do? What shall I say?" He always obeyed the Father's direction. *"Not my will be done but yours, O Lord."*

You and I not only have the written Word, but we have the guidance of the Holy Spirit within us. The Word has been given to us to teach us and train us in God's ways and precepts, but also we need answers in our individual lives: "What am I supposed to do about this problem? What am I supposed to do today? What can I do today, Lord, to please You?"

Jesus knew the written Word of God, and He operated by the voice of God. The two always agree.

In John 5:46 Jesus said, *"For had ye believed Moses, ye would have believed me: for he wrote of me."* If He had been dealing with the people who knew the books of Moses, they would have believed Jesus when He came, because Moses wrote of Jesus. But He said, *"If ye believe not his writings, how shall ye believe my words?"* (John 5:47).

Unless we believe the written Word of God, we won't follow the voice of the Holy Spirit telling us what to do. We won't believe the Spirit of God as He speaks to us, unless by the written Word we know His ways. God's ways are so high above our natural ways.

We must have the written Word in our hearts so we can learn to discipline ourselves to make the right choices and live our lives according to the Word of God. Then when the Spirit of God tells us to do something, we will be quick to recognize it as God leading us because we already know how God thinks.

When we walk with God, we must totally learn to rethink our lives because the world's way—the way we first learned to think—is foolishness to God. The world is in darkness and is backward compared to what God says and knows. *The Amplified Bible* says that the whole world around us is under the power of the evil one (1 John 5:19).

Because of this, you and I are faced with a decision. We can live in either of the two realms—the natural or the supernatural. We are born again in the spirit, so we can walk in the spirit, or we can walk after our soul (mind, will, emotions—or natural thinking). We can acknowledge God in all our ways and lean not to our own understanding, or we can continue to live like the rest of the world in permanent defeat until we leave this earth. But why choose what the world chooses when we can walk with God?

God is searching our hearts to see what is inside us. He is searching for a people who will do what He says and be dedicated to Him. Jesus is loyal to God. He lives His life for God. This same Jesus lives in us. We are His Body. He is endeavoring to get us to live totally for God. He does it. We are to do it, too.

Jesus said, *"For I came down from heaven, not to do mine own will, but the will of him that sent me"* (John 6:38). When He was on the earth, He did not live His life for Himself. He lived it loving God with His whole heart, soul and might.

Keeping the Word and obeying God's voice, Jesus also said, *"And he that sent me is with me: the Father hath not left me alone; for I do always those things that please him"* (John 8:29). Don't you know it was a delight to the Father's heart to see a man in the earth keep His Word, obey His voice and live life totally for Him? Likewise, our Father wants this to be the word of the Church today: "I do always those things that please Him."

But we need to change. And change starts with individuals—with you and me. We are members of the Body, but members in particular. God wants us to be able to honestly say, "I do always the things that please Him."

It is important to understand that Jesus laid down His life before He ever went to the cross. During His time on earth He continually laid down His life to please God. Do you think He lived an unhappy life? Did He miss out on very much because He did not seek His own will or His own interests? Did He pay too great a price to walk pleasing to God as far as the rewards of this life are concerned? Of course not!

Did He fail at anything? Yes! He never got around to committing a sin, never experienced sickness, never knew defeat. Just think how much He missed! Would you miss much if you walked the earth as Jesus did with such power, anointing and glory? No, you wouldn't miss a thing. You would walk in that same high life. God is trying to get blessings to you, and this is the way they will come to you unhindered, and in full measure—by your being obedient to the Lord and by doing what you are told to do.

Jesus walked in total victory. He put Satan down at every turn. Satan could not touch Him because Jesus was allowing God to be God in His life. The Father was an enemy to His enemy, and a friend to His friend.

Because Jesus kept God's Word and obeyed His voice, God could manifest His power through Him without measure. Jesus did not even speak His own words. Everywhere He went, if they would receive Him, He made the blind to see, the lame to walk, the deaf to hear. He delivered those who were demon possessed. The wind and the sea obeyed His voice. Every need He had was met by God's power and action.

A Unified Church

In order for God to be God in the Church like He so desires to be, we've got to obey the Word of God and follow after the voice of His Spirit. According to John 10:15-16, that is the key to a unified Body. If we can get into agreement with God, then we can get into agreement with each other: *"As the Father knoweth me, even so know I the Father: and I lay down my life for the sheep. And other sheep I have, which are not of this fold: them also I must bring, and they shall hear my voice; and there shall be one fold, and one shepherd."*

No matter where we come from or where we are in the earth, we can be united with each other. You can be on one side of the world, praying, walking in the written Word, listening to the voice of the Holy Spirit. I can be on the other side, praying, walking in the written Word, listening to the Spirit. Regardless of our location, we can be in agreement. We can be one spirit with the Lord and with each other.

If we do this, then we'll be walking under the direction of one person—Jesus. He is the Head. Our responsibility is to choose to walk in obedience so He can tell me what to do here, and can give you the same instruction there. We *can* flow together in the Spirit, even though we may not know one another—*if* we are walking in obedience to His Word and the Spirit.

The Holy Spirit is in us to bring us into this unity of the faith and into the image of the Son of God. We have been pre-destinated to be conformed to His image (Romans 8:29). There *shall* be one fold and one Shepherd! Jesus said, *"My sheep hear my voice, and I know them, and they follow me"* (John 10:27).

Oh, we have such adventure ahead of us! We have been living in the low life of this natural realm, when we could be walking in the Spirit. As God gives us revelation, we are able to walk in the spiritual realm with Him. He is revealing things to our generation to bring us to that place. He has made a way to help us be successful.

Spending Time With Our Father

Think of how Jesus spent time with His Father during His earthly ministry. He would get up a great while before daylight so He could pray. He would spend a whole night in prayer, communicating with His heavenly Father. After Jesus was baptized by John and the Holy Ghost came upon Him and anointed Him, He spent 40 days in the wilderness fasting and praying. Then the Scripture says He left that place in the power of the Holy Spirit.

As a result of His time with the Father, He knew what He was to do and He did it! He perfectly pleased God. Afterward when Satan came to tempt Him, Jesus knew exactly what to do to have victory.

We need to let Him teach us. We need to read His words as if we have never heard them before. Picture in your mind Jesus talking to you now, saying to you the same words He spoke to the disciples.

In Christian circles we have been raised in such a sloppy way with an attitude of "just get born again and live anyway you want to," that it has cost us the blessings God wants to manifest in our midst.

Getting born again is not something you just do so you will miss hell. He tells us to go win the lost, so we do it, but this is not the entire purpose of the Church. Our purpose is to please God—to be His special possession in the earth and do *whatever* He tells us to do. We should cleave unto Him, live in fellowship with Him, and be vitally united with Him. We should spend enough time with Him that we hear and recognize His voice so we *can* be pleasing to Him. When we do that, winning the lost will be the result.

Laying Down Natural Desires

In Matthew 28, Jesus told His disciples to go into all the world and preach the gospel:

> **Teaching them to observe all things whatsoever I have commanded you... (verse 20).**

In Mark 8, we read one of the most important things that He told them. Read it carefully and receive it in your heart:

> **And when he had called the people unto him with his disciples also, he said unto them, Whosoever will come after me, let him deny himself, and take up his cross, and follow me.**
>
> **For whosoever will save his life shall lose it; but whosoever shall lose his life for my sake and the gospel's, the same shall save it (Mark 8:34-35).**

In *The Amplified Bible* Jesus said it this way:

> **...If any one intends to come after Me, let him deny himself—forget, ignore, disown, lose sight of himself and his own interests—and take up his cross, and...follow with Me—continually, [that is,] cleave steadfastly to Me.**
>
> **For whoever wants to save his...life, will lose [the lower, natural, temporal life...]; and whoever gives up his life [which is lived (only) on earth], for My sake and the Gospel's, will save [his higher, spiritual life in the eternal kingdom of God].**

Now Jesus not only was talking about our going to heaven, although that is included. He also was talking about our living for Him while in the earth. To live for Him, we cannot cling to our natural lives, or the things our souls desire in the natural realm—ambition, money, recognition, or any other desires of the flesh—things that natural man seeks after with his whole heart.

He was saying, "If you will lay down your natural desires, lose sight of yourself and your own interests, you will lose that lower life. Take up your cross. Do what you are told. Follow Me and you will find that higher life."

The higher life is walking in the spirit, walking with God and walking in victory and power. It is walking and being ruled by our new reborn nature, filled with the Holy Ghost, even though we are still living in a natural body.

In Luke 18 Jesus tried to get the rich young ruler to follow Him into a higher life, but the man was unable to do it. Now Jesus did not tell everyone He met to sell what they had and give it to the poor, but He said that to the rich young ruler for some reason. The reason probably was the rich young ruler was trusting in his riches instead of God. When put to the test, he cared more for the riches.

It was of prime importance to Jesus to obey whatever the Father asked. When He was in the Garden of Gethsemane, His soul was crying out, knowing He was going to have to endure separation from God. He was so pulled by what was going to happen to Him, He prayed:

> **Father, if thou be willing, remove this cup from me: nevertheless not my will, but thine, be done.**
> **And being in an agony he prayed more earnestly: and his sweat was as it were great drops of blood falling down to the ground (Luke 22:42, 44).**

God may be telling you what to do. He may be saying, "I want you to spend more time in prayer." Perhaps you have been hearing that for weeks or months and thinking, *I really ought to do that.*

He may be prompting you in your spirit and saying, "I want you to spend more time in My Word." You have thought, *I ought to do that.* Don't put it off. Do what God is telling you. Lay down your natural desires and obey the higher calling of God.

Living the High Life

Contrary to what many Christians think, God does not begin your life of obedience by asking you to do something you're not ready or equipped to do. He's not going to send you to Africa unless you're ready. He will deal with you today, right where you are. If you will follow His leading, He will tell you what you need to do, how you need to change, what effort you need to make for Him, and where you need to go—if anywhere!

He wants us to reach the place where we trust Him, where we know He is wiser than we are, where we are willing to do what He says, whether we understand it with our minds or not. That is called walking in the spirit, living the high life.

If we hold on to our own interests, desires and ambitions— if we fight and strive to perform our own wills in the earth— the Spirit of God will have no opportunity to take us into the higher life. We never will hear His voice speaking to us, or if we hear, we will not obey. We must make the decision to lay down our lives for Him. Jesus said, "If any man intends to come after Me, let him deny himself" (see Matthew 16:24). We must reach that place where we say, "Lord, I'm giving You the rest of my time on earth. I'm living it for You."

I have made that decision in my own life. I have laid down my life before God. (And yet I have to confirm that decision over and over every day as choices are continually laid before me.) My desire is to please God and to do His will. I want to stay in the earth as long as He has work for me to do here. I am determined to run the race God has set before me, to finish my course and do it with joy! Yes, I intend to enjoy it!

But you cannot stay earthly minded and at the same time think about the glory of God, eternity, the kingdom of heaven and the Father.

Before I made this decision, there were certain things I enjoyed doing that interfered with my time with God. Those things, like hobbies for instance, were fun to me. I had to *make* myself go to the Word. Sometimes, because I so enjoyed those other things, I would spend too much time doing them, and my Word time would slide by. I have always been a reasonably disciplined person, so even in those times I stayed in the Word enough to keep my body healed and keep myself together spiritually.

Thank God, I have changed. I once had to make myself study God's Word and pray. Now when necessary I have to make myself do those other things. My interests have changed. My desires have changed. Why? Because I started paying more attention to Him and living my life for Him. I began to do everything that I felt God wanted me to do. He has taught me about following after my spirit, indwelt by His Spirit, and it has changed my life.

What did Jesus say? "If any man intends to come after Me, let him deny himself." I do not mean that I have arrived. I am just getting started, but I *am* started.

You know, this is a growing process. Growing spiritually is like growing physically. When you were born physically, your mother did not expect you to begin to talk the second day after you were born. But she would have been disappointed if you were still not talking at 5 years of age.

Spiritual things are the same way. You have to walk with God one day at a time, starting where you are today. You cannot start where someone else is. You must start where you are. But you have to start.

You will never grow if you do not give God your time. If you do not spend time in the Word and in prayer, if you do not listen to your spirit, you will never grow. You have to *do* certain things to grow.

All God asks of you is that you begin where you are today. If you do not know God, the first thing you need to do is get born again. Just make Jesus the Lord of your life and say, "I'm starting today." (There's a prayer of salvation at the end of this book to help.) Then start. Keep moving and don't ever stop!

In John 12 we find more of Jesus teaching the disciples:

> **The hour is come, that the Son of man should be glorified.**
>
> **Verily, verily, I say unto you, Except a corn of wheat fall into the ground and die, it abideth alone: but if it die, it bringeth forth much fruit.**
>
> **He that loveth his life shall lose it; and he that hateth his life in this world shall keep it unto life eternal.**
>
> **If any man serve me, let him follow me; and where I am, there shall also my servant be: if any man serve me, him will my Father honour (John 12:23-26).**

This is how you get the full blessing of God in your life—serve Jesus and the Father will honor you.

Jesus says in verse 27 in *The Amplified Bible*, "*Now My soul is troubled and distressed, and what shall I say? Father, save me from this hour [of trial and agony]? But it was for this very purpose that I have come to this hour [that I might undergo it]*."

Notice that He did not say, "Father save Me from this hour." He chose instead, *"[Rather, I will say,] Father, glorify—honor and extol—Your own name!"* (verse 28).

Just like Jesus, this is the place you and I must reach in our own lives. We, too, must say, "Father, glorify Your Name in my life. I give You my life. I give You my heart. I give You the rest of my days on the earth."

Jesus was putting this into the hearts of the disciples. Because we are also His disciples, we must have it too. *"So then, whoever of you does not forsake—renounce, surrender claim to, give up, say goodbye to—all that he has cannot be My disciple"* (Luke 14:33, *The Amplified Bible*). These were strong words, but Jesus said them. He was training His men, and He trained them well.

According to *Vine's Expository Dictionary of Biblical Words*, a *disciple* is *a learner, one who follows one's teaching*. To paraphrase Matthew 10:24-25, Jesus said, "The disciple will not be greater than his master; he will be like his master."

God has great things for those who will be obedient to Him and love Him with their whole hearts.

4

Newness of Life

What shall we say then? Shall we continue in sin, that grace may abound? God forbid. How shall we, that are dead to sin, live any longer therein?

Know ye not, that so many of us as were baptized into Jesus Christ were baptized into his death? Therefore we are buried with him by baptism into death: that like as Christ was raised up from the dead by the glory of the Father, even so we also should walk in newness of life.

For if we have been planted together in the likeness of his death, we shall be also in the likeness of his resurrection: Knowing this, that our old man is crucified with him, that the body of sin might be destroyed, that henceforth we should not serve sin (Romans 6:1-6).

We can walk in newness of life by the glory of the Father. This newness of life is our capacity and ability for obedience. We are not to walk like the world walks. We do not have to walk in death and defeat. We can walk in life and victory.

What is this newness of life? It is the life we received when we were born again—the life of God Himself.

Therefore if any man be in Christ, he is a new creature: old things are passed away; behold, all things are become new. And all things are of God, who hath reconciled us to himself by Jesus Christ, and hath given to us the ministry of reconciliation; To wit, that God was in Christ, reconciling the world unto himself, not imputing their trespasses

unto them; and hath committed unto us the word of reconciliation.

Now then we are ambassadors for Christ, as though God did beseech you by us: we pray you in Christ's stead, be ye reconciled to God. For he hath made him to be sin for us, who knew no sin; that we might be made the righteousness of God in him (2 Corinthians 5:17-21).

The Amplified Bible says a *new creation!* A new species of being that never existed before. Like a tree that never existed or a new mountain! We are not the same as we were. Now we are born of God, we have His nature and we have His Spirit. The same life God has in Himself, He imparts to us in the new birth. We don't have to live like dead men any longer. We are alive to God. We are victorious because of the life of God that's been imparted to us. Eternal life has already begun. We are not supposed to live according to the world's way or according to the dictates of our natural bodies. We are to walk after the new man on the inside created in righteousness and true holiness in the image of God (Ephesians 4:24).

We cannot walk in newness of life by giving ourselves a set of rules and regulations. We do not walk in newness of life just by telling the Church, "Don't do this. Don't do that." We walk in newness of life by the Holy Spirit as He teaches us how to walk in God's way. The Holy Spirit teaches us a better way to live—a way that works.

We who are born of God are a strange species of being! We are supernatural spirits living in natural bodies. We are alive in the spirit, yet live in a body of flesh that's subject to death. We can operate in the spiritual realm and in the natural realm. We have to learn to function in both realms in God's higher ways with this new creation in control of our flesh.

We are to know according to Romans 6:6 that the old man of sin is crucified with Him that we should no longer serve sin. *"And they that are Christ's have crucified the flesh with the affections and lusts. If we live in the Spirit, let us also walk in the Spirit"* (Galatians 5:24-25). (I capitalized Spirit because the *King James Version* does, but in the original Greek there are no capitals. The capital letters are there at the privilege of the translators. I believe this whole context of scripture is speaking about *our* flesh and *our* spirit—walking after the new reborn spirit instead of the flesh.)

We have to keep that body crucified. Paul said, *"I keep under my body, and bring it into subjection: lest that by any means, when I have preached to others, I myself should be a castaway"* (1 Corinthians 9:27). In this portion of scripture he is speaking of running the race and obtaining the prize. You won't finish the race God has set before you without keeping your body in obedience to your spirit.

When we became Christians, our old man died and we were born again. We became a new man in Christ Jesus. Just as He died and was raised from death, when we were dead in trespasses and sin He raised us up from spiritual death into eternal life. Our spirit man was raised from death into life when we made Jesus the Lord over our lives.

God did not merely allow that new nature to creep into us little by little. In one powerful moment, He removed the old nature—the heart that was full of sin and dead to Him. In one instant He replaced that old nature with the likeness of Himself.

We are born of Him. We have His nature. God lives inside us. We have received His life. We call it eternal life. It is the life of God, the substance of God Himself. We are literally His children.

As we read in Romans 6:4, Jesus Christ was raised from the dead by the glory of the Father. Just as He was raised up by the glory of the Father, so we were raised up from the dead by the glory of the Father. We passed from death to life. And we should walk in the power of that resurrection life.

A few years ago during my prayer time, the Lord dealt with me about *resurrection*. It means *rising from the dead or coming back to life; coming back into notice, practice, use, a restoration or revival; the state of having risen from the dead.*

There is coming a resurrection of our physical bodies—at the time of the catching away of the Church. But the greatest resurrection we'll ever know, we've already experienced. It occurred the moment we passed from spiritual death into spiritual life—when we were born again. That was the only death you—the real you, the spirit—will ever experience. Glory to God!

Our spirit man was raised up in eternal life. The primary part of us is not the physical body. We are a spirit being. It is the spirit that gives life to the body (James 2:26). The body is just the earthly house in which we live. When we (our spirits) leave our bodies, these bodies will die and decay, but we will be present with the Lord. One moment we are in our bodies, the next moment we are in the glory! *"Thou shalt guide me with thy counsel, and afterward receive me to glory"* (Psalm 73:24).

Now we are to put on this new man. Read carefully how we are to live this new life.

> **Since, then, you have been raised with Christ, set your hearts on things above, where Christ is seated at the right hand of God. Set your minds on things above, not on earthly things. For you died, and your life is now hidden with Christ in God. When Christ, who is your life, appears, then you also will appear with him in glory.**
>
> **Put to death, therefore, whatever belongs to your earthly nature: sexual immorality, impurity, lust, evil desires and greed, which is idolatry. Because of these, the wrath of God is coming. You used to walk in these ways, in the life you once lived. But now you must rid yourselves of all such things as these: anger, rage, malice, slander, and filthy language from your lips. Do not lie to each other, since you have taken off your old self with its practices and have put on the new self, which is being renewed in knowledge in the**

image of its Creator. Here there is no Greek or Jew, circumcised or uncircumcised, barbarian, Scythian, slave or free, but Christ is all, and is in all.

Therefore, as God's chosen people, holy and dearly loved, clothe yourselves with compassion, kindness, humility, gentleness and patience. Bear with each other and forgive whatever grievances you may have against one another. Forgive as the Lord forgave you. And over all these virtues put on love, which binds them all together in perfect unity.

Let the peace of Christ rule in your hearts, since as members of one body you were called to peace. And be thankful. Let the word of Christ dwell in you richly as you teach and admonish one another with all wisdom, and as you sing psalms, hymns and spiritual songs with gratitude in your hearts to God. And whatever you do, whether in word or deed, do it all in the name of the Lord Jesus, giving thanks to God the Father through him (Colossians 3:1-17, *New International Version).*

Dead Men Don't Sin

The old man of sin (the real man, the spirit) has already been crucified with the result that sin in the body can be overthrown. We need not sin or serve sin.

> For he that is dead is freed from sin. Now if we be dead with Christ, we believe that we shall also live with him:
>
> Knowing that Christ being raised from the dead dieth no more; death hath no more dominion over him. For in that he died, he died unto sin once: but in that he liveth, he liveth unto God.
>
> Likewise reckon ye also yourselves to be dead indeed unto sin, but alive unto God through Jesus Christ our Lord (Romans 6:7-11).

We are to consider ourselves dead to sin and our relation to it broken. We are to consider ourselves alive unto God through Jesus Christ our Lord. If you will live unto God and set your attention on Him, there is a fountain of life inside you that will flow out to permeate your mind, your body and your surroundings with God!

But if instead you live unto the world and unto sin, you will be dominated by death and defeat. It is not enough just to see ourselves dead to sin. We must *see* ourselves alive unto God.

Alive Unto God

Alive unto God. What does this phrase mean? To be alive unto God means to be responsive to His Spirit. If you are alive unto God, you will spend time in the Word of God and in prayer. You will maintain continual fellowship and communion with Him. When He speaks, you will hear and obey.

Proverbs 4:20-22 tells us that the Word of God is life and health to our flesh. So the Spirit of God will make alive our bodies. It says that the issues or forces of life come out of our hearts: *"Keep [and guard] your heart [spirit] with all vigilance and above all that you guard, for out of it flow the springs of life"* (Proverbs 4:23, *The Amplified Bible*). The *King James Version* says it this way: *"My son, attend to my words; incline thine ear unto my sayings. Let them not depart from thine eyes; keep them in the midst of thine heart. For they are life unto those that find them, and health to all their flesh. Keep thy heart with all diligence; for out of it are the issues of life."*

God says, "Consider yourself dead to sin." If you obey the Word and consider yourself dead to sin, when sin calls your name, you won't answer. You'll say, "No, I reckon myself dead to that." (In Arkansas where I was raised, you would say, "No! I reckon I'm dead to that.")

The word *temptation* means *solicitation to evil.* There will be temptations, but those temptations will not get your attention when you are dead to sin. But you cannot walk that walk without being alive to God. It is not a matter of law, but of the life of God working in you.

It is your life with God, your fellowship and responsiveness to Him, that causes sin and the things of this world to fall away from you. As you walk after the hidden man of the heart, you walk free from the sin and bondage of the world, the flesh and the devil.

Free From Sin!

Sin has lost its dominion because it's no longer inside you. You had the nature of sin but Jesus your Savior came into your life and gave you His righteousness and you, the spirit, were raised from the dead to new life. Resurrection life! The same life that raised Jesus from the dead. Sin is on the outside. It's still available to you if you choose it, but it no longer has dominion. It's not your nature. For it to have place in your life after you've been born again, you have to give it permission—you have to allow it.

Let not sin therefore reign in your mortal body, that ye should obey it in the lusts thereof.

Neither yield ye your members as instruments of unrighteousness unto sin: but yield yourselves unto God, as those that are alive from the dead, and your members as instruments of righteousness unto God.

For sin shall not have dominion over you: for ye are not under the law, but under grace.

What then? shall we sin, because we are not under the law, but under grace? God forbid.

Know ye not, that to whom ye yield yourselves servants to obey, his servants ye are to whom ye obey; whether of sin unto death, or of obedience unto righteousness?

But God be thanked, that ye were the servants of sin, but ye have obeyed from the heart that form of doctrine which was delivered you.

> **Being then made free from sin, ye became the serv-ants of righteousness.**
>
> **I speak after the manner of men because of the infirmity [weakness] of your flesh: for as ye have yielded your members servants to uncleanness and to iniquity unto iniquity; even so now yield your members servants to righteousness unto holiness (Romans 6:12-19).**

Even though we are born again, when we yield ourselves to the devil and follow after sin, we are serving him, not God. Whether a servant of sin unto death or a servant of obedience unto right-eousness, we yield ourselves to the one we are serving. We reap the harvest of the one we serve—a harvest of life or of death.

YOU let not sin reign in your body. Your body is to be ruled by you—the new creation spirit that comes from God. If your spirit were not able to handle this job, God wouldn't have given you this assignment. When God gives an assignment He always gives the ability! Your spirit, empowered by the Holy Spirit, has the power to control your body. SIN SHALL NOT HAVE DOMINION!

Yield not to unrighteousness but yield yourselves to God. You are alive to Him!

> **But if the Spirit of him that raised up Jesus from the dead dwell in you, he that raised up Christ from the dead shall also quicken your mortal bodies by his Spirit that dwelleth in you. Therefore, brethren, we are debtors, not to the flesh, to live after the flesh.**
>
> **For if ye live after the flesh, ye shall die: but if ye through the Spirit do mortify the deeds of the body, ye shall live. For as many as are led by the Spirit of God, they are the sons of God (Romans 8:11-14).**

The only way Satan has any inroad into your life is by igno-rance or disobedience. If you are born again, he has no right to any power or authority over you. You have authority and power over him. But unless you choose to live according to the Word of God and the leading of God, you will be defeated. The degree of your victory depends on the degree of your obedience.

According to Romans 8:13, the Spirit of God will teach and train us to mortify (put to death or crucify) the deeds of the body. In other words, the Holy Spirit will lead us to control our bodies to please the Lord. The Holy Spirit reveals the Word to us.

You see, God does not expect us to walk pleasing unto Him and be a glorious Church in this present world without the power of the Holy Spirit living within us. The Holy Spirit is the Great Enabler. His living within us is God's great hope for the glorious Church. His living in us is what enables us to not live like the world lives but to live with hearts open to Him. With His power enabling us we are to walk in newness of life. We are to walk in the glory—in His presence. Through Him we can...

Live a Holy Life

> ...even so now yield your members servants to righteousness unto holiness.
>
> For when ye were the servants of sin, ye were free from righteousness.
>
> What fruit had ye then in those things whereof ye are now ashamed? for the end of those things is death.
>
> But now being made free from sin, and become servants to God, ye have your fruit unto holiness, and the end everlasting life.
>
> For the wages of sin is death; but the gift of God is eternal life through Jesus Christ our Lord (Romans 6:19-23).

We have been made free from sin so that we can yield our bodies to God as servants of God in holiness.

We are to yield our bodies to righteousness unto holiness. Ephesians 4:24 says we are to put on this new man who after God is created in righteousness and true holiness.

Holy means *pure; separated unto God for divine purpose and use.* Hebrews 12:10 tells us that we are to be partakers of His holiness. First Corinthians 3:16-17 tells us we are the temple of the Spirit of God, that to defile it causes destruction, *and that the temple which we are is holy.*

Be ye not unequally yoked together with unbelievers: for what fellowship hath righteousness with unrighteousness? and what communion hath light with darkness?

And what concord hath Christ with Belial? or what part hath he that believeth with an infidel?

And what agreement hath the temple of God with idols? for ye are the temple of the living God; as God hath said, I will dwell in them, and walk in them; and I will be their God, and they shall be my people.

Wherefore come out from among them, and be ye separate, saith the Lord, and touch not the unclean thing; and I will receive you,

And will be a Father unto you, and ye shall be my sons and daughters, saith the Lord Almighty.

Having therefore these promises, dearly beloved, let us cleanse ourselves from all filthiness of the flesh and spirit, perfecting holiness in the fear of God (2 Corinthians 6:14-18, 7:1).

Ephesians 5:25-27 tells us that Jesus the Anointed gave Himself to sanctify (set apart) and cleanse the Church with the washing of water by the Word. (The Holy Spirit washes us with His Word.) He does this to present to Himself a glorious Church without spot or wrinkle, holy and without blemish. Ephesians 1:4 adds that He chose us before the foundation of the world to stand before Him holy and without blame in love. First Thessalonians 3:13 says our hearts are to be established in this holiness. First Thessalonians 4:7 says we are called unto holiness.

First Peter 1:15-16 says, *"But just as he who called you is holy, so be holy in all you do; for it is written: 'Be holy, because I am holy'" (New International Version).* Ephesians 5:1 says, *"Therefore be imitators of God—copy Him and follow His example—as well-beloved children [imitate their father]" (The Amplified Bible).*

The Bible ties the manifestation of God with our walking in holiness. Hebrews 12:14 says we are to follow peace with all men and holiness without which no man shall see the Lord. Jesus said, *"Blessed are the pure in heart: for they shall see God"* (Matthew 5:8). Romans 3:23 lets us know that sin brings us short of the glory—which is His manifested presence.

God wants His people to live a holy life because holiness is the only thing that will enjoy victory in the earth. God wants His people to live like He lives, being a total success. Holiness will bring life and peace to us.

We do as God says because His ways are our only deliverance while we live in the earth. The earth is not dominated by God's will unless the Church walks in its authority to proclaim what God says. (Do you wonder about that? Let me ask you this. Were the Dark Ages God's will? No, the earth experienced that time of darkness because the Church became, for the most part, inactive and ruled by religious tradition instead of the Word of God.)

We resist sin by the power of the Holy Spirit Who lives in us. If we do not resist, we will be swept into misery right along with the world. We will be victims of Satan's attempts to kill, steal and destroy.

Learn to speak Galatians 2:20-21 to keep your body obedient: *"I am crucified with Christ: nevertheless I live; yet not I, but Christ liveth in me: and the life which I now live in the flesh I live by the faith of the Son of God, who loved me, and gave himself for me. I do not frustrate the grace of God...."* I do not frustrate the grace (divine favor and blessings) of God. Sin frustrates God's grace because it hinders His favor from working in your life.

When temptation (solicitation to evil) comes, you have the power, authority and privilege to say, "No! I'm crucified to that. I rebuke that thought in Jesus' Name." You are resisting the devil (James 4:7). This scripture says to submit yourselves to God and resist the devil. When you're being obedient, you are submitting to God. Satan will flee. Peter says to resist the devil *steadfast* in the faith (1 Peter 5:9). He describes the devil as our adversary going around (masquerading) as a roaring lion looking for someone who will let him have place in their lives. Well, keep moving devil, I'm not the one! The Bible says give the devil *no* place (Ephesians 4:27). Take action immediately against temptation.

For though we walk in the flesh, we do not war after the flesh:

(For the weapons of our warfare are not carnal, but mighty through God to the pulling down of strong holds;)

Casting down imaginations, and every high thing that exalteth itself against the knowledge of God, and bringing into captivity every thought to the obedience of Christ;

And having in a readiness to revenge all disobedience, when your obedience is fulfilled (2 Corinthians 10:3-6).

Don't allow disobedient, immoral or wrong thoughts to linger in your mind. Immediately replace thoughts of disobedience, immorality, doubt, defeat, discouragement or fear with the Word of God.

Control your thought life with the Word of God and let Philippians 4:4-8 be fulfilled continually in your life.

Rejoice in the Lord always—delight, gladden yourselves in Him; again I say, Rejoice!

Let all men know and perceive and recognize your unselfishness—your considerateness, your forbearing spirit. The Lord is near—He is coming soon.

**Do not fret or have any anxiety about anything,
but in every circumstance and in everything by
prayer and petition [definite requests] with thanks-
giving continue to make your wants known to God.**

**And God's peace [be yours, that tranquil state of a
soul assured of its salvation through Christ, and so
fearing nothing from God and content with its earthly
lot of whatever sort that is, that peace] which tran-
scends all understanding, shall garrison and mount
guard over your hearts and minds in Christ Jesus.**

**For the rest, brethren, whatever is true, whatever is
worthy of reverence and is honorable and seemly,
whatever is just, whatever is pure, whatever is lovely
and lovable, whatever is kind and winsome and gra-
cious, if there is any virtue and excellence, if there is
anything worthy of praise, think on and weigh and
take account of these things—fix your minds on
them (Philippians 4:4-8, *The Amplified Bible*).**

Learn to think on the things of God—what His Word says
about you and your situation. Refuse to allow thoughts of sin
or defeat of any kind in your life. Live alive unto God listening
to and responding to the Word of God and the Spirit of God.
When you replace the devil's words with God's Word, you can
continually live in the blessing and favor of God.

Look at what Proverbs says wisdom (His Word) will do in
our lives:

1. **Life, healing and health.** *"For they are life to those
   who find them, healing and health to all their flesh"*
   (Proverbs 4:22, *The Amplified Bible*).
2. **Length of days and years of life worth living.** *"For
   length of days, and years of a life [worth living], and
   tranquility [inward and outward and continuing
   through old age till death], these shall they add to
   you"* (Proverbs 3:2, *The Amplified Bible*).

3. **Favor and understanding.** *"So shalt thou find favour and good understanding in the sight of God and man"* (Proverbs 3:4).
4. **Guidance.** *"In all thy ways acknowledge him, and he shall direct thy paths"* (Proverbs 3:6).
5. **Abundance.** *"Honour the Lord with thy substance, and with the firstfruits of all thine increase: So shall thy barns be filled with plenty, and thy presses shall burst out with new wine"* (Proverbs 3:9-10).
6. **Riches and honor.** *"Length of days is in her right hand; and in her left hand riches and honour"* (Proverbs 3:16).
7. **Happiness.** *"Happy is the man that findeth wisdom, and the man that getteth understanding"* (Proverbs 3:13).
8. **Peace.** *"For length of days, and long life, and peace, shall they add to thee"* (Proverbs 3:2).
9. **Security—you shall not be afraid.** *"Be not afraid of sudden fear, neither of the desolation of the wicked, when it cometh. For the Lord shall be thy confidence, and shall keep thy foot from being taken"* (Proverbs 3:25-26).
10. **Gracefulness, beauty and glory.** *"She shall give to your head a wreath of gracefulness; a crown of beauty and glory will she deliver to you"* (Proverbs 4:9, *The Amplified Bible*).

...Then these benefits will belong to us according to God's Word. God doesn't intend for us to live like the world and then pray to receive a miracle when we get into trouble. Thank God, He *will* deliver us when we get into trouble, but we are called to live so much higher than that—as high as the heavens are above the earth.

If we'll place our lives in God's hands, obey Him and begin to live that holy life, most problems will be avoided. For example, it's wonderful to receive a miracle when you're sick, but it's better to walk with God and live in divine health and stay well (Proverbs 4:20-22).

By choosing to live as a born-again believer, and by spending time fellowshiping with God in His Word and in prayer, you are choosing to open up your spirit to Him so that you can walk responsive to His Spirit—that you stay ALIVE unto God.

As you walk alive unto God, the Holy Spirit will tell you what adjustments are necessary to make you pure and holy like your heavenly Father.

So, choose life. Choose the Word—and watch the blessings overtake you.

5

A Living Communion With Him

I am the true vine, and my Father is the husbandman. Every branch in me that beareth not fruit he taketh away: and every branch that beareth fruit, he purgeth it, that it may bring forth more fruit. Now ye are clean through the word which I have spoken unto you. Abide in me, and I in you. As the branch cannot bear fruit of itself, except it abide in the vine; no more can ye, except ye abide in me.

I am the vine, ye are the branches: He that abideth in me, and I in him, the same bringeth forth much fruit: for without me ye can do nothing. If a man abide not in me, he is cast forth as a branch, and is withered; and men gather them, and cast them into the fire, and they are burned. If ye abide in me, and my words abide in you, ye shall ask what ye will, and it shall be done unto you (John 15:1-7).

Abiding is living in, settling down, dwelling in. It is not "coming in" and "going out." The *Wuest's Expanded Translation* translates abiding as "a living communion." Jesus is the vine. We are the branches. If you separate the branch from the vine, you break the union. You can lay the branch right next to the vine, but if it is not one with the vine, the life won't flow into that branch to make it produce fruit.

Rufus Mosely said, "Fruit appears on branches. God has to have branches of the same texture as Himself, the same sap, the same mind, the same spirit, before He can bring forth in fullness what He wants to bring forth." God has had to wait for a people who will be branches. James 5:7 says *"...Behold, the husbandman waiteth for the precious fruit of the earth, and hath long patience for it, until he receive the early and latter rain."*

The *Amplified Bible* says, *"So be patient, brethren, [as you wait] till the coming of the Lord. See how the farmer waits expectantly for the precious harvest from the land. [See how] he keeps up his patient [vigil] over it until it receives the early and late rains."*

Many believers don't bear fruit. They get born again, but do not abide in Him. There is no living communion—no life flow. Their spiritual lives wither and they become subject to the devil, subject to the enemy. Sickness and disease comes upon them. They do not live like spiritual men, but like natural men.

We are not to get born again and then stop. We are not born again just so God's house will be full, even though that is important to Him. We are born again to be His special possession in the earth—a group of people who will do anything He tells them to do—who will be obedient. Then He will get His plan finished and the earth will be full of His glory.

Rufus Mosely also said, "All you have to do to keep union is to put Him first and keep your mind stayed on Him. In union and love, you will have everything else. Our only responsibility is the responsibility of the union. If we will give ourselves to the union, He will look after everything else."

How are we to do this? By His Spirit. Jesus did not expect us to do that in our own power. He expected His Spirit to come and live in us and communicate His words to our spirits. The Spirit of God is in us to bring about that continual living communion with Jesus.

But the Comforter (Counselor, Helper, Intercessor, Advocate, Strengthener, Standby), the Holy Spirit, Whom the Father will send in My name [in My place, to represent Me and act on My behalf], He will teach you all things. And He will cause you to recall—will remind you of, bring to your remembrance—everything I have told you....

However, I am telling you nothing but the truth when I say, it is profitable—good, expedient, advantageous— for you that I go away. Because if I do not go away, the Comforter (Counselor, Helper, Advocate, Intercessor, Strengthener, Standby) will not come to you—into close fellowship with you. But if I go away, I will send Him to you—to be in close fellowship with you....

But when He, the Spirit of Truth (the truth-giving Spirit) comes, He will guide you into all the truth— the whole, full truth. For He will not speak His own message—on His own authority—but He will tell whatever He hears [from the Father, He will give the message that has been given to Him] and He will announce and declare to you the things that are to come—that will happen in the future.

He will honor and glorify Me, because He will take of (receive, draw upon) what is Mine and will reveal (declare, disclose, transmit) it to you.

Everything that the Father has is Mine. That is what I meant when I said that He will take the things that are Mine and will reveal (declare, disclose, transmit) them to you (John 14:26, 16:7, 13-15, *The Amplified Bible*).

In 1 John 2:20 we read:

But ye have an unction from the Holy One, and ye know all things.

The word *unction* here is the same word as *anointing* in verse 27:

But the anointing which ye have received of him abideth in you, and ye need not that any man teach you: but as the same anointing teacheth you of all things, and is truth, and is no lie, and even as it hath taught you, ye shall abide in him.

This anointing for living is from the Spirit of the God living in us. Jesus said He would lead us into all the truth. He said it was better that He went away because He would send another Comforter (the Holy Spirit) Who would live in us and teach us all things. The anointing of the Spirit of God which we have received *abides* within us. This unction of the Holy Spirit is in us continually to teach us, lead us, guide us and counsel us. He tells us what the Father and Jesus want us to do. It is just like having a two-way radio linked up to heaven. And He empowers us to do it.

> **...Work out—cultivate, carry out to the goal and fully complete—your own salvation...[Not in your own strength] for it is God Who is all the while effectually at work in you—energizing and creating in you the power and desire—both to will and to work for His good pleasure and satisfaction and delight (Philippians 2:12-13, *The Amplified Bible*).**

Now here is the catch: *"...even as it [the anointing] hath taught you, ye shall abide in him"* (1 John 2:27). What does this mean? That as this anointing teaches us, we obey. We abide in Him. Abiding is obeying. If we do not abide in Him and walk in Him, the Spirit of God is hindered in accomplishing what He has been sent to do. We either walk in obedience to our God, or we pay the price for disobedience.

The Promptings of the Spirit

> **Wherefore, my brethren, ye also are become dead to the law by the body of Christ; that ye should be married to another, even to him who is raised from the dead, that we should bring forth fruit unto God.**
> **For when we were in the flesh, the motions of sins, which were by the law, did work in our members to bring forth fruit unto death.**

But now we are delivered from the law, that being dead wherein we were held; that we should serve in newness of spirit, and not in the oldness of the letter (Romans 7:4-6).

We are to serve now in newness of spirit. *The Amplified Bible* says we serve in *"...[obedience to the promptings] of the Spirit in newness [of life]"* (verse 6). We are to serve now after this new man who is born of God indwelt and permeated by the Holy Spirit. We no longer serve the old habits and ideas we had or after the flesh that has not yet been changed. We still serve, but we serve from the inside. Now we walk in newness of life and follow the promptings of our newborn spirit as he is taught and directed by the Holy Spirit. We have died to the law that we might be married to Him Who was raised from the dead to bring forth fruit unto God.

"But he that is joined unto the Lord is one spirit" (1 Corinthians 6:17). We are to function here in the earth, even while we still live in a natural body as one with Jesus the Anointed. We were dead. Now we live to be "married" to Him.

That he might sanctify and cleanse it with the washing of water by the word, That he might present it to himself a glorious church, not having spot, or wrinkle, or any such thing; but that it should be holy and without blemish.

So ought men to love their wives as their own bodies. He that loveth his wife loveth himself. For no man ever yet hated his own flesh; but nourisheth and cherisheth it, even as the Lord the church: For we are members of his body, of his flesh, and of his bones.

For this cause shall a man leave his father and mother, and shall be joined unto his wife, and they two shall be one flesh. This is a great mystery: but I speak concerning Christ and the church (Ephesians 5:26-32).

Paul says this is a great mystery. As a man is joined to his wife and they become one flesh so is the Anointed and His Church. We are His body—flesh of His flesh, bone of His bone. We are to live united to Him as the branch to the vine so that His life and His anointing pervades every action and decision. That is the way Jesus Himself lived. He said:

> **I am able to do nothing from Myself— independently, of My own accord—but as I am taught by God and as I get His orders. [I decide as I am bidden to decide. As the voice comes to Me, so I give a decision.] Even as I hear, I judge and My judgment is right (just, righteous), because I do not seek or consult My own will—I have no desire to do what is pleasing to Myself, My own aim, My own purpose— but only the will and pleasure of the Father Who sent Me (John 5:30, *The Amplified Bible*).**

> **And he that sent me is with me: the Father hath not left me alone; for I do always those things that please him....If ye continue in my word, then are ye my disciples indeed; And ye shall know the truth, and the truth shall make you free (John 8:29, 31-32).**

The Spirit of God is the voice of God to us. He proceeds directly from the Father. The way the Holy Spirit leads us most of the time is by the inward witness. We also call it a prompting, guidance, a leading, an unction. It is an instruction in our spirits.

It is important to know that the Holy Spirit is not going to push His way into your life. Yes, He wants to lead you, but He won't force Himself into your affairs. *"For as many as are led by the Spirit of God, they are the sons of God"* (Romans 8:14).

Proverbs 20:27 says, *"The spirit of man is the candle of the Lord...."* He wants to burn His light brightly in our hearts, to illuminate our path.

The Spirit of God is within you to control your life—not by forcing you, but by leading you. He wants control of you because He is the only One on earth Who knows what to do to make your life work.

Now you might think, *I don't want anyone controlling me.*

Let's think about that. Suppose there was a human being who could answer every problem you have. You could phone this person at any time, tell him your problem and always receive the solution. You would take his direction gladly, and you would call him whenever a problem arose. That person would have control of your life with your permission. And you would be glad!

Of course, there is no natural person who knows the answer to every problem. But the Holy Spirit does! He knows all of the answers. He is in you to help you, to give you revelation and direction for your life. He wants you to call on Him. He is waiting for you to recognize Him as the Comforter (Counselor, Helper, Intercessor, Advocate, Strengthener, Standby). He is always available to come to your aid and make the difference between life and death, failure and defeat.

> **So too the (Holy) Spirit comes to our aid and bears us up in our weakness; for we do not know what prayer to offer nor how to offer it worthily as we ought, but the Spirit Himself goes to meet our supplication and pleads in our behalf with unspeakable yearnings and groanings too deep for utterance (Romans 8:26, *The Amplified Bible*).**

Many people have been filled with the Spirit for years, but never have really listened to Him. They never have learned to obey Him. They have not paid attention to the Word of God to learn how. The Holy Spirit is the Teacher, but to hear Him you will have to give Him your attention.

God is looking for people who will worship Him and serve Him in spirit and in truth (John 4:23). I realized one day that

God did not expect me to be able to do what I was called to do by my own mind or ability. He expected to give me His strength and ability supernaturally. He expected to be my portion for whatever I needed. I knew I could only please God by walking in the spirit and not in the flesh. So I prayed, "Lord, teach me to walk in the spirit," and He began to teach me. I learned things that changed my life.

The Holy Spirit will unveil His blessings to us if we will give Him an opportunity. Remember that Jesus did not become your Savior until you recognized Him as Lord and were born again. When you gave Him that recognition and allowed Him to take over your life, He became your Savior.

The Holy Spirit is the same way. He is not going to take over your life as Comforter, Counselor, Helper, Intercessor, Advocate, Strengthener and Standby until you invite Him, until you give Him place, until you recognize Him as the One Who comes to your aid and support. When you begin to listen to Him, lean on Him, rely on Him and trust in Him, He will begin to work in just that way. The more you lean on Him and not your own understanding, the more He is able to fulfill His ministry to you.

God speaks to us by His Spirit. We don't have to go to a prophet to hear from God in this dispensation of grace. We are born of God. No longer is the Holy Spirit in the holy of holies as He was in the Old Covenant. No longer is He kept in a place that is unapproachable that only the high priest can enter. He is no longer there. He is within you and me.

With the Spirit of God in us, we become mobile temples of God. Satan does not want you to know this, because he doesn't want you to realize that when you face a problem, the Spirit of God faces it with you. When you know not how to pray as you ought, the Holy Spirit takes hold together with you against that infirmity or weakness in your life and prays the perfect will of God into existence, and gives you direction that will bring victory. Then He gives you the power and ability to do whatever He directs.

Where does the Holy Ghost live? Within your spirit. God wants to talk to you spirit to spirit, and that is how His Spirit communicates with you most of the time. Usually, He does not speak directly to your mind or to your physical ears.

When you hear these promptings come up within you, you may ask, "Was that me, Father, or was it You?"

It will sound like you—and it is—because it is your own spirit that you hear most of the time. Your spirit relays to your soul (mind, will, emotions) what the Spirit of God is saying to you. It is sometimes difficult to differentiate between the two. I cannot tell you how to know the difference. I can only tell you how to get started and that you will begin to know. As you spend time in prayer and in God's Word, your spirit, which is directly infused and connected with God's Spirit, is a reliable witness to follow.

God expects you to be sensitive and to listen to the promptings—that unction, that inward witness. According to Hebrews 4:12, the Word of God divides between the soul and the spirit. It will distinguish within you between your natural mind and your spirit—between what is coming from your mind and what is coming from your spirit. If you want to walk in the spirit, you will have to spend time studying in and meditating on the Word and praying in the spirit.

The more you grow in the Lord, the more your soul will come into agreement with God. The more your soul is renewed to think like God thinks, the easier it will be for you to be led by the Holy Spirit.

We were born again in God's image on the inside, but the Holy Spirit will begin to change us on the outside as we obey Him. As we walk with Him and obey Him, the Spirit of God within us will manifest the presence of Jesus until Romans 8:29 is fulfilled:

For whom he did foreknow, he also did predestinate to be conformed to the image of his Son, that he might be the firstborn among many brethren.

As we begin to think like He thinks, the things of God will become so great that the things of the world will seem ridiculously insignificant.

Let loose the Spirit of God in your life. Walk in that anointing. Abide in that anointing. The Spirit of God is leading you, counseling you, teaching you, ministering grace to you every day of your life.

When we receive that unction from God, giving us direction, we are to obey. We are not to mentally question it. We are not to talk ourselves out of it. We are not to reason it away. (But, of course, we judge all direction by what God has already said in the written Word concerning His will and the laws of the Spirit. He will never tell us to do something that is crosswise to His Word.) When the Spirit of God rises up within us, we must act. That is what makes God able to manifest Himself in our lives, from one degree of glory to another.

Obedience opens the door that nothing else will open. Being obedient to the Spirit of God opens the door for God to honor us in full measure. God is able to work His perfect will in our lives when we honor Him, reverence Him and abide in Him. Whatever we do toward Him, we open the door for Him to do toward us. If Jesus and His Word abide in us and we maintain a living communion with Him by the Spirit of God, we'll be able to walk in continual obedience. When we do that, we put ourselves in position to ask whatever we will and it will be done (John 15:7).

Remember this: *Abiding is obeying.*

> **For yourselves, let the teaching which you have heard from the beginning abide within you. If that teaching does abide within you, you also will abide in the Son. And in the Father (1 John 2:24, *Weymouth's New Testament*).**
>
> **The man who obeys His commands abides in God and God in him; and through His spirit which He has given us we can know that He abides in us (1 John 3:24, *Weymouth's New Testament*).**

God gives us His Word. He gives us His direction. When He tells you to do something, it may seem unimportant to you. You might think it is insignificant, but your future may depend on it. God does not explain Himself. He expects you to walk by faith. He expects you to be mature. He expects you to grow up into Him so you will simply do what you are told, knowing that He is smarter than you. Then He sees whether or not we will do it. If we will not, He knows we are not ready to move on with Him.

If you have had problems in your life and you feel that God is not paying attention to you, think back to the moment you disobeyed Him last, then obey His instructions. *"Draw nigh to God, and he will draw nigh to you"* (James 4:8). He may be waiting for you to set things straight and begin again with Him.

Unless we rise up and begin to obey the anointing—the unction—in our spirits by the Holy Spirit, God will be unable to take us any further along than we are right now. Like Israel, we will stay in the wilderness until God finds another generation that's obedient. And if they accept Him at His Word and follow His Spirit, then He will take them further than He was able to take us.

We should not want to stay where we are, though it may be such a wonderful place. We must continue on so we can grow in God.

You have to start where you are right now. Obey everything that God tells you today, and then again tomorrow, and the next day. Learn to walk with God one day at a time. He will give you the grace daily for what you're to do that day. Then you will be able to look back and see a life that has pleased God. In our everyday walk we must be obedient—in the seemingly little things, as well as in the big things.

Following the Spirit of God is the only way the Church will ever do the job God has called us to do. We cannot do it in our soulish realm. We cannot operate in the supernatural and have our souls (minds, wills, emotions) in command of our lives. *We must walk in the Spirit.* To walk in the supernatural, we must be willing to go beyond what we can see with our natural eyes and walk after God by faith. We must learn to look through the eye of faith.

I made this commitment: "God, I will do anything You want me to do. Teach me and lead me."

At this time Ken did not have a daytime service, and by direction of the Lord, I started teaching on Friday mornings. (I was already teaching healing on Saturdays.) I prayed: "Father, we are just giving You this time. We are turning it over to the Holy Spirit. Whatever You want us to do, tell us."

I told the people to prepare themselves to set aside these days for the Holy Spirit to do whatever He wanted. Those services lasted sometimes for three or four hours. I just endeavored to teach the Word and to follow the Holy Spirit and minister to the people.

I said, "God, I will do anything You tell me to do. I don't care what I look like to people." If there was anyone who had cared what they looked like to people, it had been me. (Sister Etter calls this a man-fearing spirit.) I wanted to be dignified and nice. I never wanted to look foolish to anyone. On top of that I was timid, but I reached a place where it was more important what God thought about me than what people thought.

In those services God began to show me things to do and I would do them. Sometimes they would be little things, but I did my best to not hold back. It does not always have to be some big thing. God just needs to know that we will obey Him in little things before He can take us on to bigger things. *"He that is faithful in that which is least is faithful also in much..."* (Luke 16:10).

I so wanted to be led by the Holy Spirit. Here is an example of how a simple act of obedience brought me strength to be able to fulfill an assignment.

One of the things He told me to do was to lay hands on every person that had not received the manifestation of healing. I had rarely ever had a healing line and I had *never* laid hands on that many people after I had been ministering for three hours on healing. When I had finished, I was so tired I could hardly close the meeting. I had to have someone else do it.

After the next healing service, God told me to do the same thing, but at the end He said, *Now rejoice before the Lord.* Prior to that, I had said, "Lord, I will do anything You want me to do." I had not planned to rejoice before the Lord in front of all those people.

But I just turned to the musicians and said, "Let's rejoice before the Lord."

Then the Lord prompted me: *Now worship Me—spirit, soul and body. Don't just hold up your hands. Begin to dance before Me.* I had never done that and had never intended to do it. I could have thought, *I don't believe I'm ready for that yet.* But God said it, and I was so committed to obeying Him that I just began to dance before the Lord. And the people joined in with me! We were caught up in rejoicing and had a good time worshiping God.

In the previous meeting I had been absolutely exhausted after ministering. This time I had ministered about four hours when I began to dance before the Lord, and something happened in my physical body. The Holy Spirit quickened my mortal flesh and all the tiredness left me.

The Lord did not say, "If you will dance before Me, you will be rewarded for it. You will be glad you did. It will change many things in your life and your thinking." He did not say it was that important. He just said, "Do it." I was so ready to obey Him that I followed through with it. You know, it has been one of the greatest blessings I have ever known.

In previous meetings I would often be so tired that I could hardly make it to the night service. But when I began to rejoice that day, the Spirit of God refreshed me physically. Nehemiah 8:10 says, "*...for the joy of the Lord is your strength.*" That is what rejoicing is all about. All these years have come and gone and I've always had the physical strength to finish the healing service. Usually I'm not even tired!

It also did something else for me. It released me in some way from being inhibited to following after God. I became quicker to obey God in other areas that might seem foolish. It broke an inhibition that I did not even realize was there, and somehow I became freer to follow after God.

Do you know what the dictionary says *dignity* is? *Self-possession or self-respect.* I do not want to be self-possessed; I want to be Holy Spirit-controlled. But I am sure that my idea of dignity had kept me from being as free as I should be with the Lord.

Freedom happens when you follow your spirit. You do not always know what is at the other end of that act of obedience. Your primary action should be to please God. Everything the Spirit of God tells you to do will work for your good. It is *always* going to be to your advantage.

6

The Comfort of the Holy Ghost

Then had the churches rest throughout all Judaea and Galilee and Samaria, and were edified; and walking in the fear of the Lord, and in the comfort of the Holy Ghost, were multiplied (Acts 9:31).

Notice the churches were multiplied when they walked in the fear of the Lord and in the comfort of the Holy Spirit. Walking in the comfort of the Holy Spirit is walking obedient to the promptings of your newborn spirit indwelt and illuminated by the Holy Spirit. It's walking in His divine favor and blessing continually. It's having God's grace (divine favor and blessing) manifested in your life every day.

You cannot walk in the comfort of the Holy Ghost without first walking in the fear of the Lord.

Walking in the fear of the Lord is obeying Him, honoring Him, living your life according to what He says. It does not mean to be afraid of Him. It means to have such confidence in Him and respect and honor for Him that you follow Him. It means to walk in all the light you have while you look for more light.

If you walk in the fear of God, you will not do things that you know are against His will. You will not habitually sin. Proverbs 3:7 says, *"...fear the Lord, and depart from evil."* You won't say, "I'll just commit this sin, and repent later." That is having no fear of God. If you truly fear God, you will honor Him and reverence Him above everything and everyone else.

God must have priority in our lives. He should be given first place before ourselves, our families or anything else. The fear of God can never be second place. If God is second place, then we cannot be walking in the fear of Him. And if we walk in the fear of Him, giving Him the reverence, honor and respect He deserves, every area of our lives will be satisfied and multiplied. Jesus said it in Matthew 6:33: *"But seek for (aim at and strive after) first of all His kingdom, and His righteousness [His way of doing and being right], and then all these things taken together will be given you besides" (The Amplified Bible).*

All we have to do is live before our Father like little children. We must do whatever He tells us to do: "My child, let go of this thing. Make this change in your life. Put this away from you. I will help you do it. Let Me work in you."

Do you know what we need to do? Just get out of the way and let the Holy Spirit work on our behalf. When He gives us a leading or prompts us to do something, we should just obey Him like little children. We are learning to walk in a new realm—the realm of the spirit.

His Divine Favor

The Spirit of God in our lives wants to minister grace— God's divine favor and blessing—to us on a daily basis. Because of this, we can live in the continual blessing and comfort of the Holy Spirit. Grace did not stop when we were born again. When we leave this earth and go to be with Him, grace will have only begun. In the ages to come, He will lavish His grace upon us.

> **Even when we were dead in sins, hath quickened us together with Christ, (by grace ye are saved;)**
> **And hath raised us up together, and made us sit together in heavenly places in Christ Jesus:**
> **That in the ages to come he might show the exceeding riches of his grace in his kindness toward us through Christ Jesus.**
> **For by grace are ye saved through faith; and that not of yourselves: it is the gift of God (Ephesians 2:5-8).**

Salvation is a free gift of God. It comes to us by the grace of God. Salvation is more than the new birth. It is salvation in every area of our lives. *Vine's Expository Dictionary of Biblical Words* says *salvation* means *deliverance, preservation; material and temporal deliverance from danger and apprehension; pardon, protection, liberty, health, restoration, soundness, wholeness.* Our salvation does not stop when we are born again. Philippians 2:12 says, *"...work out your own salvation with fear and trembling."* In other words, have respect and honor unto Him and continue to work out your own salvation.

What does it mean to work out your own salvation? It simply means to follow after the Holy Spirit. Only God knows the end and the depths of salvation and the wonderful things He has prepared for us in this life. He has more in store for us than just going to heaven when we die. We are to live in the blessing and dominion of God while here on earth.

Let's look now at 1 Corinthians 2:

> **But as it is written, Eye hath not seen, nor ear heard, neither have entered into the heart of man, the things which God hath prepared for them that love him.**
>
> **But God hath revealed them unto us by his Spirit: for the Spirit searcheth all things, yea, the deep things of God.**
>
> **For what man knoweth the things of a man, save the spirit of man which is in him? even so the things of God knoweth no man, but the Spirit of God.**
>
> **Now we have received, not the spirit of the world, but the spirit which is of God; that we might know the things that are freely given to us of God (1 Corinthians 2:9-12).**

God's Spirit is in us to reveal the wonderful things that God has already prepared for us. The treasure house of heaven is open to us. God's communion and grace, His divine favor and blessing, is to be continually enjoyed in our lives. That is walking in the comfort of the Holy Spirit.

"The earth is the Lord's, and the fulness thereof..." (Psalm 24:1). He wants His Church—the glorious Church, His special people—to repossess this place spiritually. It does not belong to the devil. It belongs to God. Satan stole it from God through Adam's sin and disobedience. God wants us to take it back by His Spirit in obedience to Him.

Remember, by one man's trespass, death reigned. By one man's disobedience, sin reigned. But I want to announce this:

> **For if, because of one man's trespass (lapse, offense) death reigned through that one, much more surely will those who receive [God's] overflowing grace (unmerited favor) and the free gift of righteousness (putting them into right standing with Himself) reign as kings in life through the One, Jesus Christ, the Messiah, the Anointed One (Romans 5:17, *The Amplified Bible*).**

God by His Spirit is teaching us to walk with Him here so the kingdom of God can be manifested and the earth filled with His glory. We take the people of this earth from the hands of the devil as we are controlled by the Holy Spirit.

You must reach the place of trusting the Holy Spirit to fulfill His ministry. As you trust Him, He will be able to lead you. The promptings of the Holy Spirit in us will prevent us from going in the wrong direction and will enable us to go in the right direction.

The Holy Spirit ministering grace reveals God's plan for our lives. If we never walk in the Spirit, we will never walk in God's perfect will for our lives. We will just be walking in the dark, bumping against the walls of life.

The Apostle Paul in Galatians talks about our falling from grace. He is writing to the Church, to born-again people. When he writes about their falling from grace, he does not mean they are going to hell. He is referring to their falling from the position of being ministered to by the Holy Ghost on a day-to-day basis. *"I marvel that ye are so soon removed from him that called you into the grace of Christ unto another gospel"* (Galatians 1:6).

We are called to live and dwell in the blessing and grace of Christ Jesus Himself. We are joint heirs with Him. He has given us the keys to His kingdom.

> **O foolish Galatians, who hath bewitched you, that ye should not obey the truth, before whose eyes Jesus Christ hath been evidently set forth, crucified among you?**
>
> **This only would I learn of you, Received ye the Spirit by the works of the law, or by the hearing of faith?**
>
> **Are ye so foolish? having begun in the Spirit, are ye now made perfect by the flesh?**
>
> **Have ye suffered so many things in vain? if it be yet in vain.**
>
> **He therefore that ministereth to you the Spirit, and worketh miracles among you, doeth he it by the works of the law, or by the hearing of faith? (Galatians 3:1-5).**

Let's look at Galatians 5:

> **Stand fast therefore in the liberty wherewith Christ hath made us free, and be not entangled again with the yoke of bondage....**
>
> **Christ is become of no effect unto you, whosoever of you are justified by the law; ye are fallen from grace.**
>
> **For we through the Spirit wait for the hope of righteousness by faith (Galatians 5:1, 4-5).**

Here Paul said that Christ had become of no effect. What did he mean? All the wonderful things Jesus bought and paid for in redemption were having no effect in their lives, because they were no longer going after the Spirit. They were going after law, following after another gospel.

They fell from the state of dependence on the Holy Spirit— they fell from grace. The Spirit of God was unable to minister to them all the blessings of redemption, all the things God had prepared for them because they were not depending on the work of the Holy Spirit. He was unable to minister grace— divine favor and blessing—to them.

Galatians 5:4 in *Wuest's Expanded Translation* reads:

You are without effect from Christ, such of you as in the sphere of the law are seeking your justification. You have lost your hold upon [sanctifying] grace.

They were no longer seeking after the Spirit; they were seeking after keeping the law for their justification. They had lost their hold upon sanctifying grace.

What does the word *sanctify* mean? *To set apart.* Paul was saying to them, "You have lost your hold upon the grace of God by the Spirit of God that sets you apart from the world."

Most Christians have never entered into the fulness of grace in daily life because their understanding and expectation of grace stops at the new birth. They only have known enough to get born again. Most Christians do not even know enough to walk in divine health. But when they die, they will go to be with the Lord.

Galatians 5:5 in *Wuest's Expanded Translation* reads:

For, as for us, through the agency of the Spirit, on the ground of faith, a hoped-for righteousness we are eagerly awaiting....

We allow the Spirit of God to minister grace to us on the ground of faith. Faith comes by hearing the Word of God. Faith gives us access into the grace of God.

> By whom also we have access by faith into this grace wherein we stand, and rejoice in hope of the glory of God (Romans 5:2).

> For by grace are ye saved through faith; and that not of yourselves: it is the gift of God: Not of works, lest any man should boast (Ephesians 2:8-9).

What is faith? Hearing and obeying God's Word—the written Word and His Word in our hearts. Faith demands action. We must hear the guidance of the Spirit and obey it, and that obedience opens the door and gives us access to grace—the wonderful favor of God. To walk in the grace and favor of God is to walk in the comfort of the Holy Spirit.

As we cooperate with His Spirit and be obedient, grace overtakes us and we walk in the goodness of God. The moment we begin to seek Him, the Holy Spirit begins to minister grace in our lives. We would never be able to become mature sons and daughters of God without the grace of God. He could have given up on us, but His grace continued after us. He lovingly waits for us to receive that grace. He wants to bring to pass in our lives everything Jesus bought and paid for on the cross. Jesus destroyed the works of the devil. He destroyed Satan's kingdom. We have already absolutely been made free in every area of life.

Our obedience to God—obeying His voice and keeping His commandments—causes us to live in the earth like we were already in heaven. How can that be? Because heaven is in us. The Holy Spirit is in us. He is the earnest of our inheritance (Ephesians 1:14). Wherever the Holy Spirit is given dominion in the life of a believer, the kingdom of God—the dominion of God—is manifested.

Let's not be like the Galatian Christians. Christ became of no effect to them. They fell from grace—they deprived themselves of the ministry of the Holy Spirit from Whom they received daily grace for daily living. You and I need not spend one day in darkness and defeat if we will be obedient to God and listen to His Spirit.

We read in Romans 8:13-14:

> ...if ye through the Spirit do mortify the deeds of the body, ye shall live. For as many as are led by the Spirit of God, they are the sons of God.

The word *sons* in the Greek means *mature sons* of God.

> For they [our earthly fathers] verily for a few days chastened [or disciplined] us after their own pleasure; but he [God] for our profit, that we might be partakers of his holiness (Hebrews 12:10).

The Holy Spirit is here for our profit. He is here to instruct us. The word chastened does not mean He makes us sick or knocks us in the head. It means He teaches, instructs, admonishes, corrects and disciplines us.

> Thus saith the Lord, thy Redeemer, the Holy One of Israel; I am the Lord thy God which teacheth thee to profit, which leadeth thee by the way that thou shouldest go.
> O that thou hadst hearkened to my commandments! then had thy peace been as a river, and thy righteousness as the waves of the sea (Isaiah 48:17-18).

God teaches us to profit. He is in us to teach us to profit in all things, first of all spiritual things. When we profit in spiritual things, profit in the natural realm is the byproduct.

He will teach us how to be holy as He is holy. We are to be separated from the world so we live like the Father instead of like the world.

Now no chastening for the present seemeth to be joyous, but grievous: nevertheless afterward it yieldeth the peaceable fruit of righteousness unto them which are exercised thereby.

Wherefore lift up the hands which hang down, and the feeble knees;

And make straight paths for your feet, lest that which is lame be turned out of the way; but let it rather be healed.

Follow peace with all men, and holiness, without which no man shall see the Lord:

Looking diligently lest any man fail of the grace of God; lest any root of bitterness springing up trouble you, and thereby many be defiled (Hebrews 12:11-15).

We do not want to fail the grace of God. We do not want to frustrate the grace of God by not obeying the Holy Spirit.

What good is it to have a Counselor if we fail to do what He says?

What good is it to have a Strengthener if we will not receive His strength?

What good is it to have a Helper if we give Him nothing to help?

The only way He can do anything for us on a continual basis is through our obedience in following Him because we each have a will. He never imposes His will over ours. He gives us direction. He prompts us. He provides that inward witness. But we are never forced to obey. We can always go our own way and then pay the price for disobedience.

It is wonderful to know that the Spirit of God is within us. May we always be willing to hear His voice and obey Him in full measure.

Second Corinthians 9:8 in the *The Amplified Bible* says, *"And God is able to make all grace (every favor and earthly blessing) come to you in abundance...."* This would encompass every area of life. Since we first received Him, God has been ready to minister grace to us, to set us apart, to bring us to a place where He can give His blessings to us without restraint. When this happens, others know we are His special people. They see the blessings of God. They see the manifestation of His presence in our lives. It is a witness to them of His goodness.

Our Commandment Is Love

Strife will cause the grace of God to fail in our lives. Strife, unforgiveness, being critical—these things restrain the Holy Spirit from moving on our behalf. He will be hindered in blessing and favoring us, because the Spirit of God ministers grace through our obedience.

"This is my commandment, That ye love one another, as I have loved you" (John 15:12). We are to love as Jesus loved. If we don't walk in love, we won't be able to walk in the manifested grace of God on a day-to-day basis. If we fail to keep this commandment, the work of God's Spirit is greatly hindered in our lives.

If you have been praying for some specific needs, but have not been getting results, check your love life. Are you loving the people with whom you come into contact? If not, the power of God is restrained in your life because you are walking in disobedience. Until the love of God begins to operate in your life, the Holy Spirit will be unable to minister unhindered to you to accomplish in your life the good that God desires.

The Bible says when man subverts his ways, his heart frets against the Lord (Proverbs 19:3, *The Amplified Bible*). Many times we go about living the way we want and simply expect God to fill in the gaps when we get into trouble.

When trouble comes, we say, "God, why did You let this happen to me?"

God did not let it happen to you. *You* let it happen to you by being disobedient.

You might say, "Well, I didn't know any better." Then you need to become more knowledgeable. You cannot stay in ignorance and stay in blessing at the same time. Satan will cram defeat down your throat as long as you will stand there and take it.

The word *grace* means *free, undeserved favor.* The Greek word for *grace* is *charis.* When Christians believe in the gifts of the Spirit, they are called *charismatics.* What are the gifts of the Spirit? They are simply gifts of God's grace shed abroad in our midst. We don't deserve them. We can't earn them. They come at God's will. They are a manifestation of His grace. Many times a person who receives a gift will not even be standing in faith. (In this situation, someone's faith is active, but not necessarily the one who receives.) God just comes down by His grace and distributes the gifts of the Spirit as He wills. Why? Because God is good. The gifts of the Spirit are gifts of grace. God lavishes them upon us because of His goodness and His mercy.

Obeying the Spirit

As we obey the Holy Spirit, those gifts of grace will become profuse in our midst. Miracles will come to pass constantly because grace operates unhindered as we obey Him. As the Holy Spirit ministers grace, people are miraculously healed and delivered.

There are different areas of healing. Not all healing results from a gift of the Spirit. As believers, we have authority over sickness and disease. We also receive from God just because we believe and act on God's Word.

But through the gifts of healings, God personally takes care of a matter. He comes on the scene and gets the job done. He says, "Let Me take over on this one." This is the way He wants to operate in our midst. He wants us to become so obedient to Him, that He can do as He desires in the whole earth through us—and not just to the Church, but *through the Church* to those who sit in darkness.

See that ye refuse not him that speaketh. For if they escaped not who refused him that spake on

earth, much more shall not we escape, if we turn away from him that speaketh from heaven....

Wherefore we receiving a kingdom which cannot be moved, let us have grace, whereby we may serve God acceptably with reverence and godly fear:

For our God is a consuming fire (Hebrews 12:25, 28-29).

It is only through the favor of God given to us by the Holy Spirit that we are able to come to a place of obedience with Him.

You may think, *I would love to live for God. I would love to live in obedience to Him. But I know I could never do it.*

You are right. You could never do it—by yourself. But you won't have to do it alone. You have the Spirit of God to help you. Remember, He is the Great Enabler. Just take the instructions of the Lord one step at a time. Prepare your heart. Feed on the Word. Pray in the Spirit. Do as you are told, and He will work in your behalf.

Jesus said He could of Himself do nothing (John 5:19). But with the Holy Ghost's power in Him and on Him, He could do anything! He was not alone.

How God anointed Jesus of Nazareth with the Holy Ghost and with power: who went about doing good, and healing all that were oppressed of the devil; for God was with him (Acts 10:38).

Jesus was anointed with the same Holy Spirit Who anoints the Church, the same One Who lives in us. God expects us to obey His Spirit, then He will do the work. Everything we are told to do, we can do. We have the easy part. If we give Him place, He will do the rest.

According as his divine power hath given unto us all things that pertain unto life and godliness, through the knowledge of him that hath called us to glory and virtue (2 Peter 1:3).

The knowledge of God will bring us everything that His divine power has already provided for us. *"All things that pertain unto life and godliness"* are wrapped up in the Holy Spirit (see 2 Peter 1:3). As we listen to Him, hear His voice and obey, the things pertaining to life and godliness become ours in the earth.

Look at 2 Peter 1:2: *"Grace and peace be multiplied unto you through the knowledge of God, and of Jesus our Lord."* How are grace and peace multiplied? Through the knowledge of God and of Jesus our Lord. We receive that knowledge from the Holy Spirit as we listen and obey Him in the written Word and obey His prompting inside us. Isaiah 26:3 says, *"Thou wilt keep him in perfect peace, whose mind is stayed on thee...."* As we keep our minds on God, we will think about the right things, such as the Father, Jesus, the Word of God, faith, obedience, the glory of God.

We learn about God by reading and studying the written Word. We are enlightened and illuminated by the Spirit of Truth. He leads and guides us. Not only does He teach us the Word, He also reveals God's will for our personal lives. He gives us the full knowledge of God because He is God's Spirit sent to live in us and teach us the things of God.

Through listening to Him and communicating with Him, in living communion with Him, grace and peace are multiplied to us.

What is the wisest thing for you to do? Go after more of God. Pray in the Spirit. Pray with your understanding. Spend time with your Father. Read the Word and meditate on it. Think about it. Ask Him to teach you the truth. Ask Him to lead you. If you need to know something, ask Him about it. He is the teacher.

If you were a student in school and did not know what to do, you would ask your teacher. In the same way, the Holy Spirit, Who proceeds directly from God, is living in you, and He is your own private tutor—your teacher. I know it is a difficult thing to fathom. You have to receive grace to believe it. You have to allow the Spirit of God to reveal it to you. Why would you walk in the dark or live in confusion when the Spirit of God is in you? There is only one reason—failure to listen to Him and do what He says.

The Spirit of God ministers grace to us on a day-to-day basis. That makes us want to be obedient so He can manifest His blessings in our lives. The obedient are blessed of God. It always has been that way. The Apostle James wrote:

> **Ye adulterers and adulteresses, know ye not that the friendship of the world is enmity with God? whosoever therefore will be a friend of the world is the enemy of God.**
>
> **Do ye think that the scripture saith in vain, The spirit that dwelleth in us lusteth to envy?**
>
> **But he giveth more grace. Wherefore he saith, God resisteth the proud, but giveth grace unto the humble.**
>
> **Submit yourselves therefore to God. Resist the devil, and he will flee from you (James 4:4-7).**

Very often, people quote this scripture only partially. They say, "Resist the devil, and he will flee from you." First it says, *"Submit yourselves to God."* Then it says, *"Resist the devil, and he will flee from you."* Satan flees from the obedient.

By the Grace of God

> **For I am the least of the apostles, that am not meet to be called an apostle, because I persecuted the church of God. But by the grace of God I am what I am... (1 Corinthians 15:9-10).**

It was the grace of God that brought Paul to where he was in God. That same grace works in you and me. It is not that we have been so wonderful or so perfect. He has favored us! Because of grace we will go on to the place God has for us.

We have to trust in His grace. Just say, "God, I know Your grace is available to me. It is sufficient. It's by grace that I am what I am." I do not want God's grace bestowed on me to be in vain. I want to walk in that grace of God. I want Him to be able to do His perfect will in my life.

...by grace have you been saved completely in past time, with the present result that you are in a state of salvation which persists through present time, and raised us with Him and seated us with Him in the heavenly places in Christ Jesus, in order that He might exhibit for His own [interest] glory in the ages that will pile themselves one upon another in continuous succession, the surpassing wealth of His grace in kindness to us in Christ Jesus. For by the grace have you been saved in time past completely, through faith, with the result that your salvation persists through present time (Ephesians 2:5-8, *Wuest's Expanded Translation*.)

We are in a state of being made sound. Our salvation will continue to work until we come to the place in which we are predestined to live. You and I live in the permanent state of God's favor. If we will walk in obedience and listen to the Holy Spirit, He will lavish that grace upon us day by day.

Filled With and Controlled by the Holy Spirit

Ephesians 5:18 says, "*...be filled with the Spirit.*" Paul wrote this letter to Spirit-filled Christians. He was instructing them in how to live. So, what does it mean to be filled with the Spirit? The word *filled* means *to be controlled.* It is literally saying, "Be being filled. Stay filled to overflowing."

Wuest's Expanded Translation says, "*Be constantly [filled] controlled by the Spirit.*" You are to conduct yourselves constantly in the spirit—instead of in the flesh or after your soul. You are to be continually controlled by the Spirit of God as you follow your spirit indwelt and influenced by Him.

Listen to the voice of your spirit, prompted by the Holy Spirit, and begin to act accordingly. As we are controlled by the Holy Spirit, we will make the proper adjustments to the Spirit as He leads us into certain areas and tells us things to do. Do the simple things you are led to do, like witness to someone, share God's Word with someone, give someone some money or pray for someone. Do what that inward witness directs you to do in the everyday decisions and choices you face.

Include a commitment to obey God during your morning prayer, *"Lord, thank You for leading me by Your spirit today. I set myself to listen and obey. See that I don't miss one of Your directions. My desire is to follow You in all things. Thank You for Your divine favor and blessing everywhere I go today. You are always so good to me. Thank You, Father."*

If you'll pray that way, as you go through the day, you'll have supernatural knowledge come up on the inside of you that you would not have received if you had not spent time with God. The leading of the Holy Spirit is easy to miss unless you have made the decision to listen and pay attention.

When you receive that knowledge—act on it! As you do, the Holy Spirit will be able to give you grace in every situation. You'll find, as the Apostle Paul did, God's grace is sufficient for you: for His strength is made perfect in your weakness (2 Corinthians 12:9).

I learned that in an unforgettable way one morning many years ago. I was preparing to teach at the Southwest Believers' Convention in Fort Worth, studying this very subject of the grace of God, when I received a call that really hurt me. Now, I'm not very easily hurt. But this situation concerned one of my children.

When someone mistreats my children, it's hard on me. The news I received wounded my heart. I was going to have to minister in just a little while and I was really hurting. What's more, I was starting to get mad.

I would have kept right on getting madder, if it hadn't been for the leadership of the Holy Spirit. After I cried a little, I began praying in tongues and He sent one of those promptings into my spirit. *Get up on your feet and begin to praise the Lord.*

I can tell you, naturally speaking, that was the last thing I felt like doing. But I obeyed anyway. I stood up and began saying, "Lord, I worship You. I praise You." Then I jumped and praised for a little while.

Next I was impressed to read a prophecy I had been given. As I read it, I was strengthened. Finally, a scripture began to boil up inside me. *"No weapon that is formed against thee shall prosper"* (Isaiah 54:17).

Then suddenly, I realized I was free. Just a few minutes before I had been so burdened down that I felt like I wouldn't be able to minister. I felt totally unable. But now all discouragement was gone. I wasn't bothered at all. It was over!

Looking back on that situation, I can see that my obedience released the grace of God to me. If I had continued to walk after the flesh and refused to do those things the Holy Spirit prompted me to do, I would have shut off His grace for that situation. He wouldn't have been able to set me free.

Think about it! I didn't realize at the time that those little things I was impressed in my spirit to do would be the key to my deliverance. I didn't know they would open the door to God's grace. But they did! I was able to walk in the comfort of the Holy Spirit as I obeyed Him. The weapon Satan formed against me could not prosper!

The same will be true for you. Great deliverance will most often come—not by overwhelming acts of God or burning bushes—but by hearing and obeying those quiet promptings of the Spirit. Your greatest victories will come by following the quiet promptings of God and walking in the comfort of the Holy Ghost one step at a time.

Be alive unto God. Obey Him. Choose Him. Then He will supernaturally manifest His presence in your life. When you face a test or trial, you will know where to turn. You will know what to do. You will have confidence in God. You will receive the answer to whatever the situation may be. You may be tested and tried, but you will have an answer when you choose God. He is your answer!

When a negative situation arises, just continue to walk in the spirit and not in the flesh. Listen to the Lord. Make adjustments as the Spirit of God leads. Continue to do what you know to do. Be faithful. If you stay in the Word and in faith, then you will not get discouraged or depressed. You will not throw up your hands and say, "God, why did You let this happen to me?" God is on your side. Listen to Him and He will show you the way of escape (1 Corinthians 10:13).

The more time you spend with God, fellowshiping with Him, the more your confidence in Him will grow. You will have boldness before the throne of grace and before the devils of hell. You will have the assurance that you have received whatever you ask. That's believing God!

Obeying Your Spirit

Walking in obedience is continually making proper adjustments to the Holy Spirit. Be quick to hear and quick to change. If we desire to be led of and by the Holy Spirit, we have to be willing to manage our lives in such a way that we stay in living contact with Him, moment by moment. If you spend all your time on natural things, the voice of your spirit will be indistinct and covered up by those things. There is a cost to pay to be able to continually hear from God, but nothing compared to the cost of missing His direction to you. If the proper adjustment is not made on your part, the Holy Spirit is hindered in performing His ministry on your behalf.

Remember the words we use in relation to hearing from God: inward witness, leading, guidance, prompting, unction.

None of these are strong, forceful words. The number one way God leads His children is by a "witness" in their heart. Usually not a voice, but a knowing, "This is what you are to do." Christians who don't give God attention by spending time in prayer and time in the Word usually aren't able to give attention to the inward witness either. But if we walk after the things of God and learn to listen to the "knowing" that comes from our spirit into our understanding, we can walk in the light as He is in the light. We will never have to stumble in darkness. We can continually hear and obey what the Holy Spirit is saying and walk in the comfort of being controlled by Him. What a place to live!

Here is an example. Billye Brim had a friend whose son lives in Oakland, California, and works in San Francisco. These people are believers. One day in his office he had this thought, *I think I'll go home early and miss the traffic.* The World Series was being played in San Francisco at the time. From the way I understood it, it wasn't like a voice from heaven or strong, forceful or commanding. Just a "prompting." That is the way the leading of the Spirit usually is—quiet and subdued. God doesn't explain Himself; He just gives a direction. This man had a witness in his spirit. He agreed with it and left early. That was the day of the big earthquake in 1989. If he hadn't left early, he would have been on the Oakland freeway at the time it collapsed!

Making proper adjustments to what the Holy Spirit prompts you to do can save your life. Learn to be pliable in the hands of the Holy Spirit. The dictionary says *pliable* means *easily bent or molded; easily influenced or persuaded; readily yielding to influence, argument, persuasion or discipline; adaptable, tractable. Tractable* means *easily led, taught or managed.* This is exactly what we want to be where God is concerned. See yourself pliable and tractable in the hands of God.

"'For I know the plans that I have for you,' declares the Lord, 'plans for welfare and not for calamity to give you a future and a hope'" (Jeremiah 29:11, *New American Standard*). God has a wonderful and exciting plan for your life. To follow His plan we have to be easily led, taught and managed by the Holy Spirit.

In the Old Covenant Israel refused to follow God because of unbelief. In essence God said to them, "This is what the Lord says—your Redeemer, the Holy One of Israel: 'I am the Lord your God, Who teaches you what is best for you, Who directs you in the way you should go. If only you had paid attention to My commands, your peace would have been like a river, your righteousness like the waves of the sea"' (see Isaiah 48:17-18). If only you had paid attention! Church, let this not be so in our day.

If you make a quality decision to obey the written Word of God and to obey the inward witness as you hear from heaven moment by moment, you can continually enjoy a lifestyle of victory by walking in the comfort of the Holy Ghost.

The Holy Spirit is teaching and training us as we would teach and train a child because we are as little children in spiritual things. We have to become as little children to walk after the Spirit and not be afraid to make a mistake. We have to care more about what God thinks of us than what man thinks. What difference does it make what we look like to the world? What really counts is how we look to God!

7

Praying the Perfect Will of God

For so many years I walked on the written Word of God and depended on it. It changed my life. The Word renewed my thinking. I began to think like God thinks in many ways. But one area in which I was insecure was making decisions when the Word did not give me specific directions.

The Word does not tell us whether to move to another city or what person to marry. We have to make these individual decisions by the direction of God's Spirit in our spirits. We have to learn to listen to our spirit who is being communicated with by the Holy Spirit. Romans 8:16 says the Holy Spirit bears witness with our spirits.

You cannot wait until you see a burning bush or hear an audible voice to follow God. If you did, you would not know where you are going most of the time. I wish it were so plain when God talks to us that we could hear His audible voice, but that audible voice happens too rarely to rely on for everyday guidance.

Harden Not Your Heart

Wherefore (as the Holy Ghost saith, Today if ye will hear his voice,
Harden not your hearts, as in the provocation, in the day of temptation in the wilderness...) (Hebrews 3:7-8).
Again, he limiteth a certain day, saying in David, Today, after so long a time; as it is said, Today if ye will hear his voice, harden not your hearts (Hebrews 4:7).

You must be willing to hear His voice and harden not your heart. How do you harden your heart? You resist the Word of God and the promptings of the Spirit. You decide, "No, that is not my will; I have decided to go another way." You might not make that actual declaration, but if the Spirit of God leads you to do something and you fail to do it, essentially you are saying, "I shall do my own will in this matter." If you harden your heart, it is unbelief to the written Word and to the voice of the Spirit of God that comes up within you. Harden your heart and you will not live in rest.

One definition of *harden* is *to make firm, solid or rigid.* In Ezekiel 36:26, God says He will take away the stony heart and give a heart of flesh, or a soft heart, a pliable heart. You could say it is a heart that the Holy Spirit can maneuver.

So, if you harden *not* your heart, what happens to you?

> **There remaineth therefore a rest to the people of God. Let us labour therefore to enter into that rest, lest any man fall after the same example of unbelief (Hebrews 4:9, 11).**

Enter Into His Rest

Teaching His disciples, Jesus said:

> **I thank thee, O Father, Lord of heaven and earth, because thou hast hid these things from the wise and prudent, and hast revealed them unto babes.**
>
> **Even so, Father: for so it seemed good in thy sight.**
>
> **All things are delivered unto me of my Father: and no man knoweth the Son, but the Father; neither knoweth any man the Father, save the Son, and he to whomsoever the Son will reveal him.**
>
> **Come unto me, all ye that labour and are heavy laden, and I will give you rest.**

> **Take my yoke upon you, and learn of me; for I am meek and lowly in heart: and ye shall find rest unto your souls.**
> **For my yoke is easy, and my burden is light (Matthew 11:25-30).**

We should labor to enter into that rest. What is the rest of God? Walking in the Spirit. Walking in a life that is controlled by the Holy Spirit. This is the high life Jesus was talking about—walking in liberty from the bondages of this world. Nothing in this world can defeat us if we enter into the rest of God. To walk in His Spirit will make us obedient to Him, and the power of God will be manifested in us.

People's souls are so pressured in this hour. There are so many problems in the world today, so many problems in individuals' lives. Jesus was talking to us in this passage. He was saying: "Whatever you learn of Me, cause that to be the path of your life, and you will find rest for your souls."

Take His yoke upon you. It is easy. You'll love the results of obedience!

Give God Control

> **For the word of God is quick, and powerful, and sharper than any twoedged sword, piercing even to the dividing asunder of soul and spirit... (Hebrews 4:12).**

The Word of God divides the soul and the spirit. The Word of God will distinguish, clarify or separate the soul and the spirit.

When I look back in my own life, I can see how I was held back spiritually. It was not my willingness to disobey God. I have been willing to obey Him since I first began to study His Word. It was my inability to hear from God and recognize His leading that held me back spiritually. It was not through any willful determination. I just did not recognize most of the time what God wanted me to do. When I had to make a decision, I would try to figure out the best way for me to go. I didn't know how to recognize my spirit.

Thank God, that is not the way you and I have to walk. We should not walk according to our own intellect or reasoning. We should walk according to the Spirit Who knows all things. But we must make the decision to allow Him to direct our actions.

"In all thy ways acknowledge him, and he shall direct thy paths" (Proverbs 3:6).

A Word From God

Near the end of 1982 I heard a prophecy that changed my life. The Lord gave me direction and instruction. This word from the Lord impressed on me that if I would just give a tithe of my time, an hour or two a day to the Lord, all would be well, my life would be changed and empowered. At the time I especially thought about my family. I needed things well in my family.

One result of this exhortation by God's Spirit is that God led me to pray in the Spirit an hour each day. At that time, even five minutes seemed long to me. I just did not spend much time in prayer. I concentrated on God's written Word. I would go to Him, show Him His Word, believe it, act on it and it would come to pass in my life. But I had never spent much time in prayer. This word from God changed my life.

It has been more than 12 years since I decided to spend an hour or two with God every day. It has been of major importance to my spiritual growth and the well-being of my present life. I sincerely believe that all my needs are met abundantly today because I obeyed this direction. My children are serving the Lord. My grandchildren are well and happy. My children have blessed and happy marriages, and they are prospering. We are *all* well.

Ken and I are still happy and in love with each other after 33 years. I believe we have run the race God set before us and obeyed His will for our lives up to the present day. Yes, I am still spending at least an hour in prayer every morning. I like for all to be well!

But this prophecy wasn't just to me. It was to the Church. Spending time with God every day for an hour or two—in His presence: in prayer, in His Word, praising Him, in services—will change your life as well.

The important thing is to do what God tells *you* to do and to be consistent in the things of God. Spending time in eternal things is not like spending time in the affairs of this world. Your prayers are eternal, and eternal things never end. They have everlasting reward.

Praying in the Spirit

For he that speaketh in an unknown tongue speaketh not unto men, but unto God: for no man understandeth him; howbeit in the spirit he speaketh mysteries (1 Corinthians 14:2).

When I began to pray an hour each day, I prayed mostly in the spirit—in other tongues. In the spirit I prayed the perfect will of God. I was able to pray His will even though I did not know the specifics of His will about many things with my intellect. I spoke mysteries unto God (Romans 8:26). *Weymouth's New Testament* translation says "divine secrets."

Likewise the Spirit also helpeth our infirmities: for we know not what we should pray for as we ought: but the Spirit itself maketh intercession for us with groanings which cannot be uttered.

And he that searcheth the hearts knoweth what is the mind of the Spirit, because he maketh intercession for the saints according to the will of God (Romans 8:26-27).

The Holy Spirit helps us to pray the perfect will of God. He makes intercession for the saints with groanings which cannot be uttered, but He does it through us. He does not do this on His own apart from us. We must listen to Him, obey Him and allow Him to help our weaknesses.

"...*The Spirit also helpeth our infirmities.*" The word *infirmities* in the Greek is *weaknesses*. The Amplified Bible translates it this way: "*So too the (Holy) Spirit comes to our aid and bears us up in our weakness....*"

If something in your life is giving you trouble, the Spirit of God will bear you up and give you wisdom and strength to overcome it. He gives you answers. Ephesians 3:16 says, "...*be strengthened with might by his Spirit in the inner man.*" The Spirit of God works within us to strengthen our spirits—to endue us with His power so we can overcome. He not only tells you what to do, He imparts to you the strength and ability to do it.

You may have been Spirit-filled for years but have not been listening to Him or paying attention to what He has been saying to you. He will give you the answer, every answer. Whether a large problem or small problem, the Spirit will work against it. He is our Helper, Strengthener, Standby, Intercessor, Advocate, Counselor, Teacher. He is on our side! Romans 8:31 says, "...*If God be for us, who can be against us?*" You could say, "If God be for us, what difference does it make who is against us!"

When He prays the will of God through you, He goes to the exact root of the problem. You and I might only realize the symptom. He deals with the cause. Thank God, there is nothing too hard for Him. And if you care about it, He cares about it.

Often we don't know how to pray as we ought. But the Spirit of God knows. The Spirit of God is in you to pray through you—to give you utterance in the perfect will of God. That is what praying in other tongues is all about. He prays God's answer through you. Praying in the Spirit overcomes the weakness you have because of lack of knowledge as well as the weakness you have because of living in a natural body. It helps your spirit to receive enlightenment and strength to dominate your actions.

"He that speaketh in an unknown tongue speaketh not unto men, but unto God: for no man understandeth him; howbeit in the spirit he speaketh mysteries" (1 Corinthians 14:2).

Jude 20-21 says, *"But ye, beloved, building up yourselves on your most holy faith, praying in the Holy Ghost, Keep yourselves in the love of God, looking for the mercy of our Lord Jesus Christ unto eternal life."*

Romans 8:27 reads, *"And he that searcheth the hearts knoweth what is the mind of the Spirit...."*

He makes intercession for the saints according to the will of God. God looks on the heart, and you look so much better in your heart than in your flesh. But He wants you to look as good on the outside as you look on the inside. Following after the Holy Spirit will bring that to pass. Following after the Word of God and the leading of God in your spirit will cause you to be conformed to the image of His Son (Romans 8:29).

In our hearts we must desire to please God. We must despise things in our lives that we know are not right before Him. As born-again believers, we do not want to sin. We want to be free. We want to please God.

The problem we've experienced has been getting our souls and bodies in agreement with our hearts. The Word of God and praying in the Spirit is the answer. We must give ourselves over to the Spirit of God, begin to pray in the Spirit, and allow the washing of the water of the Word to present us a glorious Church not having spot or wrinkle or any such thing and without blemish (see Ephesians 5:25-27).

You may ask, "But can't I pray in my own language?"

Yes, but not to the degree you need to be praying. You can only pray with your own understanding according to the knowledge you have. Many times you will not know enough in the natural to accurately pray for the answer, but the Holy Spirit inside you will provide God's solution when you pray in the Spirit. The Holy Spirit prays God's higher way into the situation—His perfect will.

We should pray both ways the Apostle Paul said:

> **For if I pray in an unknown tongue, my spirit prayeth, but my understanding is unfruitful. What is it then? I will pray with the spirit, and I will pray with the understanding also: I will sing with the spirit, and I will sing with the understanding also (1 Corinthians 14:14-15).**

The Holy Spirit is in us to bring to pass the will of God in our lives. Bringing to pass God's will is the preeminent responsibility of the Church in the earth. Because the Church is made up of individual people, this responsibility starts with you and me. Each person in the Church standing before the Lord, being obedient to the Spirit of God, will cause God's will to be done in the earth.

We are favored to be able to pray with the understanding and with the spirit. We do not know enough in our natural minds to be that glorious Church without spot or wrinkle, but in the spirit realm we do. We must reach down into our spirits that are indwelt by the Holy Spirit and find out what to do. As we take our place in the spirit, God's special people will rise up in the earth.

What if We All Prayed in the Spirit?

Now think of all the different people it takes to make up the Body of Christ in the world today. What if we all prayed an hour each day in the Spirit? How many hours of praying the perfect will of God would that represent?

Once the Body of Christ rises up and becomes obedient to God, with each individual doing what he is told, we will reap the harvest of souls that God desires—and we will do it quickly!

God might tell one person to pray five hours. Someone else may be told to pray 15 minutes. The important thing is that we do what we are told. I was told to pray an hour each day, and it has changed my life. (Now I pray in English as much as in the Spirit—just whatever direction I receive.)

If you prayed in the Spirit one hour a day, by the end of the year you would have prayed 365 hours of the perfect will of God. Just 15 minutes a day would be 91 hours. Don't you think that would affect everything in your life for good? It certainly did mine. I wouldn't consider not spending time in prayer every morning.

I want you to realize that God will deal with you right where you are today. He might tell you to pray five minutes each day. He may ask you to start there and then increase. Five minutes is important when you are praying the perfect will of God. It is God praying through you. He gives the utterance, you give Him your authority and your voice. When you pray in the spirit, your intellect will not get in the way because you are not praying out of your head, but out of your spirit.

We must come to a place where we keep God's Word, obey His guidance and simply do what we are told—a body of people that God can depend on to do His will in the earth.

What God said exactly was "Don't take up all your time with natural things...but see to it that you give heed unto your spirit and give your spirit opportunity to feed upon the Word of God...and give your spirit opportunity to commune with the Father above and build yourself up on your most holy faith...just an hour or two out of 24, just pay a tithe of your time unto Me, saith the Lord and ALL WILL BE WELL."

8

Becoming the Glorious Church

So where are you in your walk of obedience? Are there adjustments you need to make? Are you ready to go on with God? Are you ready to *be* that glorious Church? I am.

Paul said in Romans 12:1-2:

> **I therefore beg of you, please, brethren, through the instrumentality of the aforementioned mercies of God, by a once-for-all presentation to place your bodies at the disposal of God, a sacrifice, a living one, a holy one, well-pleasing, your rational, sacred service....**
>
> **And stop assuming an outward expression that does not come from within you and is not representative of what you are in your inner being but is patterned after this age; but change your outward expression to one that comes from within and is representative of your inner being, by the renewing of your mind, resulting in your putting to the test what is the will of God, the good and well-pleasing and complete will, and having found that it meets specifications, place your approval upon it *(Wuest's Expanded Translation)*.**

Paul said to put your bodies at the disposal of God and stop assuming an outward expression that does not come from within us. In other words, we've got to stop being hypocritical. We usually consider a hypocrite to be someone who is wrong on the inside and tries to look right on the outside. He talks a certain way but is not really that way. *This scripture is speaking of a believer who is right on the inside, but acts wrong on the outside.*

It is a lie for us to live like the world when we are born again. We are not like the world when we are born again. We are like God, and we are to live like Him. God says to us, *"I'm holy—you be holy. Separate yourself from the world."*

We should look like God. We must change our outward expression by allowing that which is within us to come out. We have to allow the glory in us to be revealed. This happens by having our minds agree with God and allowing Him to express on the outside of us what He has already done on the inside of us.

Ephesians 4:17-23 in *Wuest's Expanded Translation* says:

> **This, therefore, I am saying and solemnly declaring in the Lord, that no longer are you to be ordering your behavior as the Gentiles order their behavior in the futility of their mind, being those who have their understanding darkened, who have been alienated from the life of God through the ignorance which is in them, through the hardening of their hearts, who, being of such a nature as to have become callous, abandoned themselves to wantonness, resulting in a performing of every uncleanness in the sphere of greediness.**
>
> **But as for you, not in this manner did you learn the Christ, since, indeed, as is the case, you heard and in Him were taught just as truth is in Jesus, that you have put off once for all with reference to your former manner of life the old self who is being corrupted according to the passionate desires of deceit; moreover, that you are being constantly renewed with reference to the spirit of your mind.**

We are not walking in the futility of our souls, but in the newness of spirit. We are no longer alienated from the life of God. It is within us so we can walk after that newness of life instead of the darkness of the world.

Being God's Special People—
That Glorious Church

For the grace of God that bringeth salvation hath appeared to all men, Teaching us that, denying ungodliness and worldly lusts, we should live soberly, righteously, and godly, in this present world; Looking for that blessed hope, and the glorious appearing of the great God and our Saviour Jesus Christ; Who gave himself for us, that he might redeem us from all iniquity, and purify unto himself a peculiar people, zealous of good works (Titus 2:11-14).

God is not a quitter. What He starts out to do, He will accomplish. He is so patient that He continues to work age after age to get His will accomplished. He will not stop until He gets this earth restored to the way it was when He originally made it, until He brings the restitution of all things in the earth.

The perfect will of God is the glorious Church. We are indeed becoming that Church without spot or wrinkle, having been washed by the water of the Word and cleansed before God. When we know the perfect will of God and begin to walk there, all nations will recognize it. When the glory of God is manifested in our midst, the whole world will know it.

God is working toward that end, and you and I are His special people. He is counting on us to keep His Word and obey His voice so He can bring that plan to pass in the earth. We are vital to God's work. The Church of Jesus Christ holds the future of the world.

The Spirit of God—even though He is here on the earth—is hidden inside you and me. He lives in us, and until we begin to obey God and cooperate with His plan, the Spirit is for the most part hidden to the world. The world sees the Holy Spirit, Jesus the Savior and God the Father through the Church.

"But he that is joined unto the Lord is one spirit" (1 Corinthians 6:17). We are one spirit with Him—one spirit with the Lord. Verses 19-20 read:

What? know ye not that your body is the temple of the Holy Ghost which is in you, which ye have of God, and ye are not your own? For ye are bought with a price: therefore glorify God in your body, and in your spirit, which are God's.

We are the temple of the Holy Spirit. He lives in us! You are to glorify God in your body and in your spirit which belong to God. We are a redeemed people. We are a purchased people. We are a peculiar (special) people, a royal priesthood. We have been bought with a price (1 Corinthians 6:20)—the blood of Jesus. He paid for us with the sacrifice of Calvary. We don't belong to ourselves. We belong to God. What a wonderful privilege to belong to God—to be His sons, His daughters.

But ye are a chosen generation, a royal priesthood, an holy nation, a peculiar people [a treasure unto God]; that ye should show forth the praises [virtue] of him who hath called you out of darkness into his marvellous light (1 Peter 2:9).

Acts 2:17-18 says God will pour out of His Spirit in the last days upon the servants and the handmaidens. The word translated *servants* and *handmaidens* means the same thing. One is the female gender and one is the masculine gender, but the word means *bondslave.* He will pour out His Spirit upon the bondslaves—upon those who have given up their will to His will.

Jesus though a son was a servant of the Father. He only did what the Father told Him to do. He did not even speak His own words.

You and I are born-again children of God. We choose to serve. God will not force us. We serve Him of our own free wills.

Jesus laid down His life to serve the Father. He is telling us to lay down our lives to serve Him, to become one who gives up his will for the will of another—like a handmaiden or a servant. Those are the ones upon whom God is going to pour out His Spirit. They will prophesy, and there will be signs and wonders.

We have a great future, both individually and as a Church, if we will follow after God and do in our lives what He says to do—instead of following our natural desires. We will find that the more we do what He says, the better our lives will be.

You will never be free unless you follow God. It is not what you and I want to do that counts. It is what God wants us to do. We can think of many good things to do with our lives, but these count for nothing in the sight of God. Unless we begin to walk in the spirit and follow after the Spirit of God, we will never come to that place where we know His perfect will for our lives.

I'm Ready to Go On!

The word from God I referred to earlier caused me to drop less important things in my life to go after the things of God. It caused me to turn my attention to God's Word. Another part of that word talked about a spiritual army. The Holy Spirit exhorted that if we wanted to be a part of this army to purpose in our heart: not to be lazy, not to draw back, not to hold back or sit down, but to rise up, march forward and become on fire!

I wanted to be a part of the move of God. I wanted to be in that army of the Lord. I made adjustments in my life and began to march forward. I chose to run the race God has set before me and win!

9

From Glory to Glory

Let's look at 2 Corinthians 3:18 in *Wuest's Expanded Translation*:

> **Now, as for us, we all, with uncovered face, reflecting as in a mirror the glory of the Lord, are having our outward expressions changed into the same image from one degree of glory to another according as this change of expression proceeds from the Lord, the Spirit, this outward expression coming from and being truly representative of our Lord.**

As we look into the glory of God, live unto Him and have our souls renewed to allow that glory to change us on the outside, our outward expression will be changed into the same image from one degree of glory to another. It is a process that we are going though.

We must allow God to be God over our entire being—spirit, soul and body. Yield yourselves fully to the Holy Spirit. Live your life for God. Do what He tells you to do, whether you feel like it or not. Cause your will to be conformed to His Word. When you come to that place, the glory of God will be manifested in you. You will be yielded to the Holy Spirit. The things of God are not hard. You just have to know how He thinks and then flow with Him. You cannot do it on your own.

In Matthew 17 Jesus took Peter, James and John to the Mount of Transfiguration. Verse 2 in *Wuest's Expanded Translation* says:

> **And the manner of His outward expression was changed before them, that expression coming from and being representative of His inner being. And His**

face took on a different appearance so that it shone like the sun, and His outer garments became white like its light.

What happened to Jesus on the Mount of Transfiguration? The glory of God was revealed in Him. That which was inside Him began to show on the outside. It was not dropped upon Him from heaven. It came from inside Him. His outward expression changed to display His innermost being. The glory of God radiated through His body and through His clothing until He shone like the light of the sun.

We are being changed from glory to glory, from one degree of glory to another. As we allow the inner man to come into dominion over the outer man, the new creature in Christ Jesus will take over the life of the outer man. The outward expression will be changed. As Romans 12:2 tells us, "Don't be conformed to the world, but be transformed by the renewing of your mind."

How are we going to be transformed? We will be transformed by the Spirit of God when we renew our minds. And our minds are renewed by the Word of God.

We can't transform ourselves. God is the only One Who can transform us. In fact, we can't even really change ourselves in a lasting way that will cause us to be transformed into His likeness. If that is true, then how can we change? What can we do to be transformed into His likeness?

This is an area where so many believers have felt frustration and failure. How many times have I heard Christians say, with sincere tears, "I've tried so hard to change but I just can't seem to do it. I go along pretty good for a while, doing what I should, but something inside isn't any different. And eventually I end up no better off than I was before. Where am I missing it?"

You don't change yourself by human power. You just commit to the Word, come into agreement with that Word, act on the Word and the Spirit of God will change you. When you commit yourself to hear and to obey the Word of God, the power of God through His Word will change you. Your desires will change; you will begin to desire what God wills. The glory of God revealed in you through His Word will absolutely transform you.

Let's look at 2 Corinthians 3:18 again. I particularly like the wording in *The Amplified Bible:*

> **And all of us, as with unveiled face, [because we] continued to behold [in the Word of God] as in a mirror the glory of the Lord, are constantly being transfigured into His very own image in ever increasing splendor and from one degree of glory to another; [for this comes] from the Lord [Who is] the Spirit.**

When you stop struggling to transform yourself by your own fleshly efforts and just commit yourself to God's Word, through the process of time you'll look up one day down the road and discover that you're different. You'll discover that your way of thinking has changed and worldly habits of the flesh have fallen away. Mortifying the flesh won't be the struggle it once seemed when you yield to the transforming power of His Word. The Apostle Paul said:

> **For I reckon that the sufferings of this present time are not worthy to be compared with the glory which shall be revealed in us (Romans 8:18).**

The glory of God was placed in you when you were born again. Second Corinthians 4:7 says, *"We have this treasure [glory] in earthen vessels...."* God wants to bring it to the surface, so it can be revealed to the world. As we pursue God's Word and yield to His Spirit, walking in the Spirit will become a way of life to us. We will get to the place where His glory will continually be revealed in us. Walking with Him will become as natural for us as breathing. And that is the very thing the heart of God has desired for so long.

You have the Spirit of God within you. Jesus is your Lord.
Walk with the Lord. Obey His voice. Prepare your heart. Feed
upon His Word. Listen to the Spirit of God as He speaks to
your spirit. As you do, your mind will be changed to think in
line with what God thinks. You will accept the great and
mighty move of the Spirit of God as it comes in our day.

You will allow God to flow out of you in a supernatural way.
The changing of your mind will allow the Spirit of God to take
dominion in your life. You will flow in the supernatural as
easily as a bird flies in the air, as naturally as a fish swims in
water, as simply as you breathe air. Do you think about
breathing? No, you just breathe naturally. In the same way,
you will not be conscious of your faith or the power of God at
work within you. The supernatural will become the natural
way of life for you. It will not seem far out to you as you walk
in the Spirit. It will not be unnatural when signs and wonders
start happening in your midst. You will be more conscious of
what is going on inside you. You will be more conscious of the
flow of the Spirit of God as He manifests Himself. You cannot
push a button and cause Him to be manifested, but you can
walk with Him on a day-to-day basis. That is your part.

God does the changing. He changes your mind so that the
supernatural is a natural way of life to you. He gives you a part
to play and that part is your responsibility. The rest is up to
Him. You pray and study the Word and obey. He will change
you from one degree of glory to another by His Spirit.

God has made us a special people, formed for Himself. We
take His Word and put it into our lives. We obey regardless of
tradition or what man thinks. We are a people who care more
for what God thinks, than for what man thinks. We deeply
desire to please God and to come into His complete will for
our lives. We dare to believe God. When we hear His voice, we
harden not our hearts. We are quick to obey. We walk after
His Spirit.

WHAT A GLORIOUS CHURCH! KCM

Prayer for Salvation and Baptism in the Holy Spirit

Heavenly Father, I come to You in the Name of Jesus. Your Word says, *"...whosoever shall call on the name of the Lord shall be saved"* (Acts 2:21). I am calling on You. I pray and ask Jesus to come into my heart and be Lord over my life according to Romans 10:9-10. *"If thou shalt confess with thy mouth the Lord Jesus, and shalt believe in thine heart that God hath raised him from the dead, thou shalt be saved."* I do that now. I confess that Jesus is Lord, and I believe in my heart that God raised Him from the dead.

I am now reborn! I am a Christian—a child of Almighty God! I am saved! You also said in Your Word, *"If ye then, being evil, know how to give good gifts unto your children: HOW MUCH MORE shall your heavenly Father give the Holy Spirit to them that ask him?"* (Luke 11:13). I'm also asking You to fill me with the Holy Spirit. Holy Spirit, rise up within me as I praise God. I fully expect to speak with other tongues as You give me the utterance (Acts 2:4).

Begin to praise God for filling you with the Holy Spirit. Speak those words and syllables you receive—not in your own language, but the language given to you by the Holy Spirit. You have to use your own voice. God will not force you to speak.

Now you are a Spirit-filled believer. Continue with the blessing God has given you and pray in tongues each day. You'll never be the same!

Books by Kenneth Copeland

*   A Ceremony of Marriage
    A Covenant of Blood
    A Matter of Choice
    Faith and Patience—The Power Twins
*   Freedom From Fear
    From Faith to Faith—A Daily Guide to Victory
    Giving and Receiving
    Healing Promises
    Honor Walking in Honesty, Truth & Integrity
    How to Conquer Strife
    How to Discipline Your Flesh
    How to Receive Communion
    Love Never Fails
*   Now Are We in Christ Jesus
*   Our Covenant With God
*   Prayer—Your Foundation for Success
    Prosperity Promises
    Prosperity: The Choice Is Yours
    Rumors of War
*   Sensitivity of Heart
    Six Steps to Excellence in Ministry
    Sorrow Not! Winning Over Grief and Sorrow
*   The Decision Is Yours
*   The Force of Faith
*   The Force of Righteousness
    The Image of God in You
    The Laws of Prosperity
*   The Mercy of God
    The Miraculous Realm of God's Love
    The Outpouring of the Spirit—The Result of Prayer
    The Power of the Tongue
    The Power to Be Forever Free
    The Troublemaker
    The Winning Attitude
*   Welcome to the Family
*   You Are Healed!
    Your Right-Standing With God

*Available in Spanish

Books by Gloria Copeland

*   And Jesus Healed Them All
Build Yourself an Ark
From Faith to Faith—A Daily Guide to Victory
God's Success Formula
*   God's Will for You
God's Will for Your Healing
God's Will Is Prosperity
God's Will Is the Holy Spirit
Harvest of Health
Healing Promises
Love—The Secret to Your Success
No Deposit—No Return
Pressing In—It's Worth It All
The Power to Live a New Life
*   Walk in the Spirit

*Available in Spanish

Other Books Published by KCP

Heirs Together by Mac Hammond
John G. Lake—His Life, His Sermons, His Boldness of Faith
Winning the World by Mac Hammond

World Offices
of Kenneth Copeland Ministries

For more information about KCM and a free catalog, please write the office nearest you:

Kenneth Copeland Ministries
Fort Worth, Texas 76192-0001

Kenneth Copeland
Locked Bag 1426
Parramatta
NEW SOUTH WALES 2124
AUSTRALIA

Kenneth Copeland
Post Office Box 830
RANDBURG
2125
REPUBLIC OF SOUTH AFRICA

220123 MINSK
REPUBLIC OF BELARUS
Post Office 123
P/B 35
Kenneth Copeland Ministries

Kenneth Copeland
Post Office Box 15
BATH
BA1 1GD
ENGLAND

Kenneth Copeland
Post Office Box 58248
Vancouver
BRITISH COLUMBIA
V6P 6K1
CANADA